On Hallowed Ground

A Gettysburg Writers Brigade Anthology

Edited by Ayleen Gontz

A division of AIM Publishing Group

ON HALLOWED GROUND

Published by Legacy Publishing, a division of AIM Publishing Group.
Gettysburg, Pennsylvania.

Printed in the United States of America.
First printing: November 2022.

PUBLISHING GROUP

315 Oak Lane • Gettysburg, Pennsylvania 17325

On Hallowed Ground

Featuring stories by:

James Rada Jr.
Mark Greathouse
Robert Scappini
Lisa Gregory
Kerry Springle
Felicia Valasek Rizzo
Greg Spicka
Patricia Parks
Judith Cameron Seniura

Edited by Ayleen Gontz

Don't Miss the Other

Gettysburg Writers Brigade Anthologies!

CONTENTS

This is the third anthology of short stories written by members of the Gettysburg Writer's Brigade. Each story relates to Gettysburg, the biggest and most historic little town in central Pennsylvania. It bears saying again that thousands of tourists come to our tiny piece of the world each year. They come seeking inspiration from the rolling hills and gentle valleys; a landscape shaped by blood; sweat, and tears; a place etched in the eternal memory of Americans and folks from around the world. The town is for many an engine of inspiration and creativity, a muse of thoughts and words, a place that holds solemn and spiritual energy for those seeking to shape ideas on paper or canvas.

The Writer's Brigade was organized in January 2010. A group of local writers willing to meet weekly to share and discuss the writing process, writing techniques, publishing, promotion, and marketing and to help our developing authors work through all these endeavors. We have over a hundred members, although, at any weekly meeting, attendance currently runs from 10 to 15. Our membership spans the gamut from novice writers with ideas for stories to published authors. In the beginning, I was the only published author and our attendance weekly was much smaller. As time has passed, I am proud to say over 50 percent of those who attend regularly are published.

In case you want to join us, we welcome new members with open arms. There are no rules for membership, only a passion for writing. We routinely meet at O'Rorke's Eatery and Spirits in Gettysburg, on Wednesday nights. We owe this amazing venue to the gracious sponsorship of our hostess, Jamie Miller, the owner. Jamie provides a warm, wonderful place for us to eat and perhaps share the occasional libation while sharing "writerly" ideas.

The Brigade would like to acknowledge Jim Rada, Ayleen Gontz, and the rest of the Anthology Committee, but it would be remiss not to mention that the entire Brigade membership contributed their encouragement and support to those who submitted their stories. Also, many thanks to Jamie and her entire staff at O'Rorkes Eatery for their kind service and overwhelmingly friendly attitude.

We hope you delight in reading the stories herein as much as I am certain our authors enjoyed writing them.

AVRAM'S BROTHER

BY LISA MURRAY GREGORY

Drifting

In rustling streams
Of brown and gold
Over slippery-moss rock
Human spirits flow

And in hearts stir
A tribal dance
A prayer for rain
The journey of their souls to enhance

To drift on
Into the waiting grasp
Of Neptune or Jesus Christ
Or whoever he or she may be
The power that stirs the calm of the sea of humanity.

—Lisa Gregory

I didn't really smell the honeysuckle until I was 82 years old.

I hadn't truly been able to smell, see the vibrance of colors or hear the glory of a melody until then. Not that I couldn't actually smell or see or hear, mind you. It was just that it was muted. My mind and my emotions had been distracted and removed from my heart and had been that way most of my life.

You see, my brother lost his life on the battlefield at Gettysburg and in doing so took mine with him.

I was five years old when my brother, Avram, went off to war, or more precisely, the Civil War. I loved my big brother and idolized him as only a little brother can do. He was 13 years older than I was, and I thought all he did and said was amazing. So did my parents.

I recollect him standing tall and proud on the day he left. I have this memory of looking up at him towering above me. I pointed out his funny cap. "Part of my uniform," he informed me as he tousled my hair in that affectionate way that brothers do.

At that moment in a desire to be like him, I wanted a cap like that. But had I known as a little boy what wearing a cap like that would mean, I might have had second thoughts. I know I have had plenty of them since.

I missed him when he left. But from what I would hear from my parents as they sat in the parlor and talked, Avram was doing something very important and dangerous.

"He's doing right by his country," my father would say, his voice full of false bravado while the look on his worried face betrayed him.

"Just pray God he stays safe," my mother would say, clutching a hand to her chest and fighting back tears.

After Avram left we heard bits and pieces of news about the war, and sometimes Avram would get a letter or message through. But mostly we were isolated on our farm and could only imagine what was happening in the greater world. Then one day, a couple of years after Avram had left to fight, it all came crashing down on us.

I was feeding the chickens when we got the news. Avram, we had last heard, was heading to a little town called Gettysburg to fight. That morning I was engaged in a battle of my own with a rooster who took unbridled pleasure in chasing me around the yard as I attempted to feed the flock.

"Ornery cuss," I whispered under my breath as I made a kicking motion at him. He just stared back at me with those beady eyes and not giving up an inch. In response I made sure to scatter the chicken feed opposite his direction and as far away from him as I could.

"Take that," I spat at him.

"Augustus! Augustus!" I heard my mother call out shrilly from our front porch.

Probably going to get a switching for teasing the rooster, I thought to myself. "But Ma," I was prepared to argue, "Old Glory started it. You know what a hateful old rooster he is. Always trying to peck at me."

My mother spotted me and hurried over, clutching a piece of paper to her chest and sobbing. I was startled.

"Where's your Pa, Augustus?" she asked between gasps for breath and tears streaming down her pale face.

I said nothing put pointed to the far field where I knew Pa was checking on one of our cows, Missy, who was about to calf. I was afraid to speak. At seven years old I understood the delicacy of the moment. That words spoken now could break the crystal-like atmosphere keeping my Ma upright and shatter her into a million tiny desperate pieces right before my very eyes.

So, I stood there in silence with my arm raised and my finger pointing to the field. Then all of a sudden, she collapsed to the ground in a pile of misery. My Pa heard her screams of agony all the way to the far edge of the field.

Avram was dead.

A fellow soldier had written a message which had arrived months after the battle. He had scrawled on a ragged piece of paper stained with blood and sweat and dirt: "Yur son has been killt."

Avram, or the earthly shell of him, would never return home. During a time when so many would never be notified of the fate of their loved ones, we were lucky. Except we weren't.

Everything changed that day.

By remaining alive I was left to fill the void left by Avram. At least by those who lived outside my home. For a young child it was an overwhelming prospect and one that I was woefully inept to accomplish. How does one compete with a ghost? The rest of what Avram's life could have been was a clean slate and my parents and others could write anything they wanted and imagined on it.

Me? I was flesh and blood.

It was a slow realization as I grew. From the weeping words of women behind lace handkerchiefs—*You are all they have now. You are the only light left in their dark world. Pray that you can bring them comfort and make up for your brother's loss*—to the men who would look over at my father awkwardly and say under their breath, *I guess that youngest boy will get the farm now.* If he ever heard them, my Pa never responded. I knew early on that I would never be prepared or more importantly be worthy enough to step up and till the land owned by my father. That had been Avram's right.

But what they didn't understand was that I was an oddity, you see. I came later to my parents— "unexpected," my mother would say. Sometimes I felt that they both resented me. I was the last in a line of seven children with only myself and Avram surviving past the first year or so.

My brothers and sisters were laid to rest at the far end of our yard with five little crosses marking their graves. I sometimes saw my mother head to those little crosses when Avram and my father were working in the fields or had gone into town and she was alone.

"Hello, my little loves," she would say cheerfully as she sat on the ground before the crosses, her skirt billowing around her.

She looked as if she were a nursery school teacher with her class of the dead. She told them Bible stories and sang them nursery rhymes. She would stop sometimes and stroke the grass that sprouted up from their graves with delicate fingers as if caressing the chubby, dimpled arm or leg of a toddler.

In my place hiding under the porch, I would close my eyes, gather up my knobby knees to my chest and pretend she was telling stories and singing to me.

But she never did. As I grew older, I began to realize that it wasn't that my mother didn't want to love me, but that she couldn't. I would sometimes catch her looking at me with a puzzled and—Dare I say it?—annoyed expression on her face. By the time of my own birth Avram was already growing into young manhood. He had beat the fate of our siblings. I was still growing. I often wondered if by loving me she felt she would risk losing me. Who was I? Who was this intruder? And how long would I stay before I too joined the row of little crosses? So, both she and my Pa put all their love, hopes, and dreams into Avram.

After my brother went away to fight and died, I was more like a shadow than a real boy. I lurked around my parents and within call if they needed something, say a chore. But just out of the way of hearing a tearful sigh from my mother or feeling a strong fist my father planted against my cheek as the object of a rage I wasn't responsible for but took the brunt of.

My Ma took to her bed after getting the news about Avram. And shortly after she emerged, she found her way to the little line of crosses in the yard. In fact, she went there even more than before. That was until my Pa came up upon her unexpectedly one day. From my viewpoint under the porch, I had seen him standing off to the side of the yard as he watched her quietly. I shuddered. He was scrunching up his eyes in that way he did when he was a might mad.

"Goddamn it woman," I heard him suddenly bellow as he stomped over to her. I pulled my knees closer to my chest and lowered my head as if preparing for a blow myself and cowered farther back into the shadows underneath that porch.

"Stop this foolishness! Stop it now!" I heard him yell as he grabbed her by the arm and drug her up the steps and into our house.

She was blubbering her apologies between deep, heart-wrenching sobs. "Just miss the little souls," she said to him as he violently pushed her through the door. "Miss my babies. Miss my Avram. Where is he? My boy buried somewhere all alone and forgotten! He should be here lying beside his brothers and sisters!"

Not a few minutes later, my Pa came out of the house swinging an ax. He went over to the row of little wooden crosses and plunged the ax deep into each and every one of them, splintering them to pieces.

"Knew this wasn't a good idea," he said in heavy breaths as he rose the ax over his head and down again and again.

When the last little wooden cross had been shattered to smithereens, he stopped and wiped the sweat from his eyes, still heaving to catch his breath. "Boy!" he shouted. "Boy! Where are you? I know you're slinking around here somewhere. Always hovering like a damn ghost. Get over here and help me pick up this wood for kindling."

That night I watched as he stacked the fire in our fireplace high with the kindling from the little wooden crosses. I couldn't help but wipe a tear or two from my grubby cheek as I sat in the glow of the fire and watched my brothers and sisters go up in smoke. Now they too were as gone from me as Avram whose remains were so far away on that battlefield at Gettysburg.

Ma stayed put in her and Pa's bedroom for the next couple of days. And when she finally emerged, I made not to notice the bruise on her cheek, the imprint. That was Pa's hand that had done that. I was well acquainted with his fisted hand and the blows it could land on a body.

With Avram's death my mother's grief was formed in keening and an almost constant stream of tears. How could one body shed so many tears? My father's grief took the shape of rage. Just pure angry rage. He had never paid much mind to me. And I tried sure to avoid him at all costs since we got the news of Avram. My Pa was looking for someone to take out his pain on and I was a constant target.

But there were times when I sought him out in hopes of

winning his acknowledgment, not even his approval, just recognition that he had another son. I never will forget the day I saw my name in a schoolbook. It was all about Roman emperors, including Emperor Augustus.

I ran home excited, and when I met up with my Pa working in the barn, filling the animal stalls with hay, I blurted out, "Did you know my name is the same as Emperor Augustus of Rome? Isn't that something?"

"Boy, you ain't no king and you ain't from Rome," my father grumbled as he spread the hay about, his work shirt soaked through with sweat. "Now get over here and help me."

"Emperor not king," I said disdainfully as I put down my schoolbooks and joined him in his task. But not loud enough for him to hear me. I was smarter than that.

Pa wasn't just angry at me. He was angry at God himself. I think my parents thought that after giving up five little ones, God had shown mercy on them with Avram. They held their breath as Avram grew. And when it seemed he would live to adulthood, my mother took out the family Bible and wrote beside Avram's name, "our beloved."

Pa wasn't a religious man. Too busy working the farm, he would say, when Sunday morning came around. Personally, I think he was probably still feeling the effects of 'shine from the night before. Pa did like his moonshine. But as Avram grew, people told how he started going to church with Avram in his arms and later holding his little hand as father and son made their way to a bench.

I think in his heart Pa made a deal with God. And now God had reneged on it. Sometimes in the deep of stormy nights lying in bed when his heart was heavy with Avram's loss, Pa swore to himself that he could hear God laughing at him, chortling away in the belly of the big booms that shook the very foundation of our house and my father's soul.

When he lost Avram, Pa, who had always enjoyed his drink, not only walked away from the church and God but also took to the drink even harder. During the evening when he first began throwing them back, I didn't mind so much. He would get all pie-eyed and soft especially around Ma. The rage would come later as he descended more and more into oblivion.

My mother had been a beauty as a young girl to hear folks tell it. She had long, thick, chestnut hair that when unpinned hung way below her waist and light blue eyes that I imagined sparkled in her earlier years. "An angel you are," my father would say to her when his friend Whimper Ellis came by with some homemade brew and they would commence a night of drinking and storytelling.

Stumbling lightly, he would make his way over to my mother, seated by the fire, her hands busy mending clothes or shucking beans to cook for tomorrow's supper. Ma wasn't one for folding her hands in her lap and being still and all. His eyes bright and dewy, my Pa would lean over and snuzzle in to try to give her a kiss.

"Stop it," she would say, pulling back from him and his alcohol breath. But from where I sat in the dark corner, alone, outside of this circle of their familiarity, I would grin to myself. She might push him away, but as he stumbled and grumbled his way back to the kitchen table and more drink, the swiftest of smiles would flicker across her face. Made me wonder what life had been like between them before the babies and death and Avram and me.

Pa's favorite drinking buddy during those times was Whimper. Folks said Whimper got his name because he was born whimpering and not squalling like most babies. Had weak lungs, they said. And he would be known to have coughing fits and lose his breath. But he made good 'shine. The whole area swore by Whimper's moonshine.

When my Pa and Whimper got to drinking and talking, Whimper always, and I mean always, told the story about his old, one-eyed mule, Helen, and a failed delivery of 'shine.

"I was taking 'shine into town," he would say as he began the familiar story at my father's urging. "Had the mason jars strapped up on Helen really good in the side bags. "

In town, he had to stop at the courthouse to "take care of some business," he said with a grin.

He had tethered Helen up to the post outside the courthouse. "Well, I guess old Helen got tired of waiting while I was doing my business inside," he would say as his grin grew bigger.

Whimper came out to see that Helen had decided to lie down and roll back and forth in the dust of the road as animals are wont to do. Probably working out an itch, I figured.

"Broke every one of my damn bottles of 'shine," Whimper would say, slapping his knee. "Damn stream of 'shine trickling down the dirt road and turning that dust to mud. My own little stream of 'shine!"

The two men would then hee-haw before taking another slug of drink.

I guess Whimper wasn't too worried. He could always make more. And a good story could be worth its weight in shine. Not a bad investment as Whimper certainly told it often enough.

Whimper would be dead just a few years later. He was making a "special delivery" to a man who was not at home at the time. And Whimper was shot to death when the husband came home unexpectedly and caught Whimper crawling out of the couple's bedroom window. The community mourned his loss, of course, but I'm not sure in doing so they were mourning the loss of the man as much as his 'shine. Whimper made some mighty fine 'shine folks would always say. Real shame they would say.

Pa might not have gone to church after Avram died, but Ma and I did. Ma said it brought her closer to God and more importantly closer to Avram. "I will see him again," she would say with her voice so full of longing you could almost reach out and touch it.

Sunday School was the last place I wanted to be on a beautiful spring or summer morning with the sun shining bold and bright in the sky and beckoning me to run and whoop in celebration of it.

At least on those glorious days we children sat outside under a big oak tree while Miss Lucy did the Sunday School lesson. She was a skinny woman with mousy brown hair pulled up in a tight bun and mousy features to match. She was what Ma called a spinster. Never married. Probably never would be.

She liked to talk about the Lord and share the parables in the Bible in an attempt to influence "impressionable young minds," as she called it. To be honest, I wasn't very impressed. I often went somewhere else in my head. Daydreaming, I guess, you would call it.

Not that Miss Lucy could tell.

During prayers in which Miss Lucy droned on and on asking for the good Lord's blessing on everyone and everything, I would tilt my head to the sky and gaze upward at the world that awaited me there. Looking at the branches and leaves of the big tree and the dappled sunlight that spread through them I would break into a big grin at the pure joy of it all.

I must have looked transfixed.

"Oh, look at Augustus," Miss Lucy would say smiling ear to ear and interrupting her prayer while softly clapping her hands together in delight. "He is full of the glory of the Lord. No doubt praying for his brother Avram's soul."

I wasn't. But she didn't need to know that.

And that's where I first spied him. Jesus boy. He looked like the picture of Jesus Christ in our church. Reddish hair like me. Blue eyes like me. But he was my age and didn't look nary as serious and dull as he did in the picture hanging at the front of our church.

As Miss Lucy prayed on, I would watch him perched on a big limb and peering down at me. Sometimes he would beckon me up silently, reaching out a hand with an impish grin. Tempting me to no good while encouraging me to ignore the prayer and climb up that big old tree. I loved it when Jesus boy came to visit during Sunday School.

Then one day he followed me home.

Me and Jesus boy became fast friends. We climbed trees and skipped rocks at the creek as well as cupping our hands together in an attempt to scoop up minnows and crawdads as we splashed about. Jesus boy never really talked and sometimes he looked sad. I understood. A lot was expected of him too.

With Jesus boy I didn't feel so alone. On that farm with just my Ma and Pa and the occasional farmhand, I now had a friend of my own.

The years went by, and I grew into manhood. My parents kept me fed and housed and clothed but that was the extent of it. Grieving can take a toll on folks, and they both were busy grieving in their own ways without much time for or interest in me.

Then when I was 18, I met Jilly. A little spitfire of a thing with dark curls and deep brown eyes. She wasn't no bigger than a minute. Her body was small, but her personality was big. She smiled, giggled and darted around me like a firefly when we were together. This time unlike the times Miss Lucy thought I was praying and feeling the glory of the Lord during Sunday School I truly was transfixed.

She delighted in the fact that my brother Avram had fought and died in the war. She was courting a real hero's brother in her mind. And when Jilly introduced me to her family for the first time, I tried to stand a little taller and force a grin and shake their hands when I was introduced, and she excitedly told them about Avram. All the while I avoided looking them in the eyes, not wanting to see their looks of suspicion and even disappointment. It was a habit I had developed early on and soon after Avram's death. The only one that I could look eye to eye was Jesus boy. And by that time, he was long gone.

Jilly and I were wed. And Jilly soon became pregnant as a young bride will do. We unfortunately had a boy.

"We are going to name him Avram," she said, glowing as she cuddled the newborn bundle in her arms with his pink scrunched up face peeking out of the small quilt that swaddled him.

I stood at the end of the bed, dropped my head and agreed. "In honor of your brother," she added, grinning ear to ear. She didn't need to clarify. I knew. I always knew.

Later that night, I packed a few things and headed out of there never to return. I left behind my parents, my wife, my baby boy, and what I hoped was any reminder of Avram and the disappointment that came with his loss. Jilly was better off without me. They all were.

I took to the drink much like my own father. When I drank I could forget, and forgetting can be a wonderful gift for those suffering. But by morning's light my memory would always return and I sought out the drink again.

During those years I was a drifter. I slept in the woods. I slept in dirty alleyways in small dirty towns. I even woke up one morning in a hog pen with the mama and her piglets snuffling at my face. I got beat with brooms if I found myself passed out in the doorway of a general store of some respectability. I begged for coins. I stole when I had to. All for the drink.

This went on for years and years. I wished for death, but it never came. I don't recall much during that time. My memory is fuzzy. I cannot, to this day, remember whole chunks of my existence. Maybe that's for the best.

It was while attempting to steal some eggs from a henhouse on a farm outside of the latest town I was travelling through that I met Libby. I was drunk and hungry. I had staggered way too far out of town and was preparing to collapse on the side of a dirt road when I saw the farmhouse up ahead.

Eggs. Straight from the nest. My mouth watered and I continued on.

As I came to the henhouse, I fell on my belly and crawled beneath the fence that attempted to protect the hens and their eggs. I looked about as I got closer but didn't see a rooster. I remembered how mean they could be. Old Glory with his beady eyes and eagerness to peck at me flashed into my mind.

I made my way inside, stirring up the dust and low and

behold took to sneezing. Couldn't stop it for the life of me. The hens started flapping and cackling. No doubt they were on the alert for a fox or a weasel but instead got a drunkard who was sneezing his dang head off.

"Who goes there?" I heard a woman's voice ask. "I swear I will shoot you."

I rose to my feet and turned around to see the barrel of a rifle pointing at me just a few feet away.

"Evening ma'am," I snickered, still under the influence of drink, weaving a bit and seeing two of her.

"Who are you?" she said, raising the rifle even higher and stepping closer.

"Just hungry," I said my senses suddenly coming to me as I threw up my arms in surrender. "Not causing any trouble."

"We'll see about that," she huffed. Then she put the gun down to her side and looked me over real good and huffed to herself again.

"Follow me," she said to my surprise as she turned and headed toward the house.

That day I became Libby's. She provided me a bath and I cleaned off the years of gunk—from dried puke to the dust and dirt of the alleyways and woods and even the chicken shit that I had crawled through in her own chicken yard.

After she had heated up water for the old wooden tub three times, mind you, because the water was so filthy from me, she threw me a blanket to dry myself and cover my nakedness. She disappeared into a room and came back with neatly folded and clean clothes. Men's clothes.

"Here." She set the overalls and shirt on a nearby chair. "I'll see about finding you shoes. Your feet look a might big. But we'll see."

I dressed quickly. My head was a little light and I wasn't

sure if it was because I was sobering up a bit or that I was having a strange reaction to being clean and covered in clean clothes instead of filth for the first time in recent memory.

"This should do," she said, returning with boots. A tad small but wearable. And then she set about making me a meal. And those eggs I had intended to steal and slurp down raw were cooked up nice for me with a hunk of salted pork.

I gobbled it up like a man possessed.

And coffee. Good lord, how long had it been since I had had a decent cup of coffee? It was black as coal and hot as hell, but it was delicious. I slurped it down so fast that I damn near burnt my tongue off.

"You will stay here," she said to me as she poured me a second cup, setting it on the table instead of handing it directly to me as my hands had now begun to tremor. My body calling out for the drink.

"You sure?" I asked as I glanced around the room to see if there was any drink available.

"And no drink," she said as if she could read my mind.

I agreed. And I never left her house. Not that giving up the drink was easy, and I had days of sweats and chills with my whole body trembling like the devil himself had grabbed hold of me and was shaking me into nonsense. I swore during those times I looked the old demon right in the eyes. Hallucinating, Libby called it. I wasn't so sure.

But it got better. And I was tired. Tired of the life I had been living these past 20 years or so. I was nearing my 50s now. Maybe it was time for a change. So, I figured Libby's was as good as any place to settle. She seemed to agree.

I would learn that Libby was alone on her farm. Her husband dead. No children. But she made that little farm hum with productivity—a garden for putting up canned vegetables, a hog each year for slaughtering in November, and of course hens and their eggs. She even had an old cow who supplied us with our milk and butter. Life was good.

Libby was a hard worker. And much to my relief she didn't ask a lot of me. Just my company, it seemed. I never knew why she took me in, and we never talked about it. I guess womenfolk like to fix things whether it be darning a hole in a sock or taking in a broken man and restoring him to health and good measure.

I respected her. But I wasn't attracted to her. She was a rotund woman as wide as she was tall. Her long face contradicted her frame, with eyes too small and close together and a beak-like nose that brought to mind images of Old Glory. And just like Old Glory, her eyes could go dead cold if you upset her. I tried not to upset her.

What she didn't have in looks she made up in cooking. Lord that woman could cook. In the dead of winter right before the planting of spring when the pantry was nearing empty, she could stretch corn pone and salt meat as well as Jesus had with his loaves and fishes. I never went hungry at Libby's.

Her man had been Jessup. He survived the war, unlike Avram. But he came back injured as many did. His left arm had taken a shell and had to be sawed off in hopes of saving his life. But it never healed right, rotting and oozing yellow and green pus and smelling to "high heaven," Libby would say, shaking her head and scrunching up her face in disgust.

Libby and I grew old together. And those were good years. There were brief moments of peace with Libby. Sitting on the back porch, eating tomatoes just picked from the garden and still warm from the sun. We'd bite into the red orbs greedily, juice dripping down our chins. "Needs some salt," I'd say.

"Eat it and be grateful," she'd tell me.

I was. And not just for the tomatoes. I had a roof over my head. Clean clothes on my back. And food in my belly. Sometimes I missed the drink but considered it a fair trade to give it up in order to live in bland contentment with Libby.

But most important of all, she never asked me about my past. The present seemed good enough for her. I gloried in that fact. For once in my life I could pretend that Avram had never existed.

Not that I didn't wonder about Libby's own past. Especially that dead husband.

"I know you wonder," she said to me one evening as she was putting the Bible away, her reading aloud finished.

"Wonder what?" I grunted back, as I spit a stream of tobacco juice into the spittoon.

"I didn't kill him," she offered. "But I wished I had," she added, looking down at her hands resting in her lap. "He was bad off. That stump never healed right. Stunk to high heaven. He took to the laudanum. And then when that didn't work anymore, the morphine."

She closed her eyes as she remembered that hot summer day when Jessup held her by the neck demanding "his medicine." I listened as Libby told her story and talked like she had never talked before. Sometimes folks just need to get things off their chests, I guess.

I was in the kitchen shelling fresh garden peas for our supper that night.

"Where's my medicine," he bellowed as he stormed into the room. "Where is it, Libby?"

He stomped over to me and grabbed me by the neck as I remained sitting.

"I ain't got it," I croaked as his hand tightened on my neck.

"It's all gone, Libby. All gone. What am I going to do? Help me. Please."

He stepped back and took his hand from my neck. I tenderly rubbed the place that would no doubt tomorrow carry his fingerprints in black and blue.

"The doc gave you some the other day," I said, softly.

"All gone," he said. He stomped around the room looking about wildly. He slung open and slammed shut drawers and cabinets.

"I know you hid some from me, right?" His tone was more hopeful than accusatory. "Always worried I'm taking too much."

"No one touches your medicine, Jessup, you know that," I said, as I gingerly rose from the table and stepped toward him, trying to catch his crazed eyes. Hold him steady. Hold him fast until the moment passed. If only God it would.

But he wouldn't look in my eyes. His mind was racing as his eyes darted around the room.

"I got an idea," he said. "Hurt myself. Not real bad. Just kind of."

He broke into a wide grin. His mood instantly changed. "Yeah, that's it."

He was mumbling now as he made his way out the door. He turned back abruptly, "Gonna need your help, Libby."

"Help with what?" I asked, wringing my hands.

"Might hard to just shoot yourself especially if you got just one arm," he said. It came off as more of a threat than a suggestion. Yet, he still grinned. This idea had offered him

relief. Respite. Even if briefly.

"No, no, Jessup," I blurted out as I backed away and against the wall. "What are you thinking?"

"Please, wife, help me. Shoot me right here in the side. The fleshy part. You've skinned enough deer and rabbit and such to know that it won't do much damage." He was pointing to his side and continuing to grin madly. "They will have to give me the morphine if I am injured. Right? Right?"

"I can't," I blurted out and ran upstairs.

"Damn coward!" he called out after me.

"Those were the last words I ever heard him say," Libby said, tears brimming in her eyes. Libby never cried. It unsettled me.

"Not much later I heard a gunshot," she continued. "I ran out to the barn. Saw him there. He lay dead on the barn floor."

Her voice faded away. Then under her breath she said, "He must have missed the fleshy parts."

She paused and then more to herself than to me said loudly and with more resolve, "Fool."

I developed a new appreciation for Libby that day. Not because she couldn't do it. But because she felt guilty that she couldn't. We never spoke of it again, which was our way.

In 1938 I got word that President Roosevelt was planning a big celebration for the 75th anniversary of the Battle of Gettysburg. Veterans from that war—both sides—would be there. And, I told Libby, "I'll be there too."

She raised an eyebrow as she kneaded dough for biscuits at the kitchen table but said nothing.

I was 82, looking at the end of my life and taking stock of things and putting things in their rightful place. That included

Avram. I hated him for what he had taken from me. I was finally going to take back what should have been mine all along. My life.

I will be honest with you, my plan was to go and visit the place where my brother had died and spit on the ground—and his grave as it were—where he had taken his last breath. I was tired of Avram and all that I wasn't and never would be. I needed to put it and him to rest and on my terms.

Yes, I know spitting on that battlefield seems a bit ridiculous. Even childish. But I needed a physical release of the pain and frustration that had haunted me all my life. A tangible release of what I had held inside me for so long. An act of revolt. A first and last act of defiance.

The morning I left to board a train for Gettysburg, Libby stood at the door and handed me some cold biscuits and salt pork wrapped up in a cloth. "For the journey," she said

I took them and nodded in appreciation as I began a journey that I hoped would change my life. Or, at least give it back to me.

I arrived at Gettysburg and stood and listened to the speeches and observed all the hullabaloo. I saw the old men and a flash of what a young Avram might now look like came into my mind. The ceremony was kicking up a big fuss with the old soldiers staying in specially assembled encampments and Mr. Roosevelt dedicating a new monument, the Eternal Light Peace Memorial.

But I couldn't help but notice that some of the old men, the veterans, while polite and maybe even appreciative, had a sadness in their eyes. I didn't ponder it too much. I was here on a mission.

I made my away from the crowds, moving slowly and breathing heavily in the hot July heat. This was no task for an old man. But I was determined.

"Goddamn it Avram, you are going to get yours," I whispered to myself as I trudged along on the uneven landscape, watching my feet so I wouldn't trip.

Finally, I stopped at the edge of the field. Here was as good a place as any, I thought to myself as I looked around. I cleared my mind and stood on that field and readied myself. I took a deep breath, gathered up a good glob of saliva and prepared to spit. I reared up, puckered my lips... but I couldn't.

Instead, I began sobbing as I fell to my knees.

This was the place where my big brother took his last breath. Avram came to me then. That big, towering brother of mine with the funny cap and the warm smile, looking down at me with love.

Here he wasn't the ghost or the constant memory that he had been at home when I was growing up. Avram had been one of thousands upon thousands upon thousands who never came home. Here on this sacred ground as they called it, he was mine and mine only. Brother to brother. No Ma or Pa to whisper in my ear that I would never measure up. No townsfolk praising him over and over and looking at me with unfair hope and expectations in their eyes and later disappointment. No baby boy who bore his name.

Just me and him. Me and Avram.

And an old friend.

For just a moment I thought I saw from the corner of my eye Jesus boy, except he was a grown man now. He was smiling at me. I hadn't thought about Jesus boy in years. And I continued to sob thinking of him and his fate as well.

Yes, I loved Avram. I had forgotten that. I had missed him when he was gone. And standing there on that field with just Avram's memory, I became overwhelmed. I was angry that Abram had left me. Left me behind. I didn't want to be him, but I had wanted to be with him.

I closed my eyes for a moment and imagined him on that hot summer day amid the chaos of war that surrounded him. The screams and gun and cannon fire. He was so young. And probably so afraid. My brother. My big brother who perched me on his shoulders and carried me about as easily if I were a feather and who wrestled with me in the yard finishing with tickles that had me both laughing and crying at the same time. My brother who had told me ghost stories as we sat around a campfire about Hidebehinds, or Hideybehinds, as we called them lurking in the woods at night and sneaking up upon you when you least expected it. He would always pull me closer to him if I got too scared from his stories.

"Don't worry Gus, I ain't ever going to let anything happen to you," he would say. "I'm your big brother and that's what big brothers do—take care of their little brothers."

But he never got that chance.

"Sorry Avram," I whispered to the wind. "Sorry you didn't get to live."

As I got to my feet and wiped the back of my hand across my face to remove the tears from my cheeks, I got a whiff of something. It stopped me in my tracks as I inhaled deeply. It was honeysuckle. The very smell of summer.

I breathed it in deeply again. Ah, that scent. Where had it been all these years? Tears threatened again, but I held them back. That will be enough of that slobbering and carrying on today, Augustus, I said to myself.

I looked up to the sky and the wonder of its majestic expanse. I could hear the faraway sounds of a harmonica—no doubt one of the old-timers, a veteran of this bloody battle, was playing some long-ago tune. It took my breath away.

Where had I been all these years? My senses were wide open. I felt like a newborn babe discovering the world around me.

I had had moments of clarity in more recent years, especially since coming to live with Libby, but nothing like this. The whole world and all that was in it opened up to me. My body felt lighter. That lead cannonball that had been sitting on my chest for most of my life had been dislodged. I felt free.

I turned around to look for Jesus again, wanting to share my newfound joy with my old friend. But he was gone. Then I suddenly remembered a Bible passage that Miss Lucy, the old spinster, had taught us in Sunday School.

"Forgive them father for they know not what they do."

Jesus said it while dying on the cross. My childhood friend. He understood. Now I did too.

"Forgive them for they know not what they do," I quoted the verse under my breath as I held the words close to my heart.

And maybe they didn't. Ma and Pa. Forgiveness can be a powerful thing.

Suddenly a voice called out to me. "Hello, there!"

I turned around quickly, wiping at my teary eyes again.

It was an old man. He was ancient looking with his scraggly beard and suspenders. He was leaning heavily on his cane but making good time nonetheless. My God, had he walked all the way over here too? I thought to myself. I was knocking at mortality's door but this man was stepping over the threshold.

"Had to get away from all that fanciness and important

goings on," he chuckled, his pale blue rheumy eyes twinkling. "Needed some place quiet to remember and say goodbye for the last time."

For a few moments he looked past me at something that I could not nor would ever be able to see. Then suddenly his mood shifted back, shaking it off like you would a chill that came out of nowhere. He turned his attention back to me.

"You fight here?" he asked.

"No," I replied. "My brother Avram did."

He nodded curtly. I felt he knew instinctively that Avram had never come home.

"A damn shame," he said, looking down. "A damn shame all of it."

And it was. For so many of us. For all of us.

But at the age of 82 I had decided that there would be no more fighting with the past. No more regrets. I was marching forward.

At that moment, I stood tall and looked the old man directly in the eyes.

"It's good to meet you," I said, offering him my hand in introduction. "I am Augustus."

Then taking a deep breath and exhaling it slowly, I added with full conviction, "Avram's brother."

Lisa Gregory is an experienced journalist whose articles have appeared in publications nationally and internationally including the *Washington Post* and *U.S. News and World Report*. She is a frequent contributor to magazines such as *Celebrate Gettysburg Magazine*, *Frederick Magazine*, *Hagerstown Magazine* and *Carroll Magazine*, among others. In her spare time Lisa is a Washington Capitals hockey fan and enjoys supporting her son's band Ignite the Fire.

A Soldier's Silence

By Bob Scappini

President Dwight D. Eisenhower searched his desk, lifting and moving files and papers to no avail. He detested confusion, and his desk in no way represented the order of things he wanted. The object of his search was a notebook with all of his thoughts and planning for the cabinet meeting next week. He would be damned if he had to do it all over again.

"That's it," he said to himself.

"Mrs. Chapman... Mrs. Chapman!"

Ann Chapman, the president's personal secretary, grabbed her steno pad and hurried into the Oval Office.

"Yes, Mister President?"

"Mrs. Chapman I can't find my notebook, you know the brown leather one, the one I've been using. It has all of my notes for the cabinet meeting next week."

"Yes, sir, let me check my reference log."

"Thank you Ann."

Eisenhower sat down and lit a cigarette. He was still getting used to the volume of information he was expected to digest on a daily basis. In the army he had a cadre of junior officers that he could rely on to feed information to him.

Now he had to carry the burden alone.

Mrs. Chapman returned with a sheet of paper.

"Mr. President, you last had the notebook when you went to the farm."

Ike rubbed the top of his head. "Damn, I remember now. Last weekend when I went up. I left it on my desk. Thank you, Mrs. Chapman."

"Sir, do you want me to send someone to get it?"

Ike leaned forward and put his elbows on the desk. "No, no, that's ok. Oh, tell me what my schedule looks like for this Saturday and Sunday."

Mrs. Chapman opened her planner and consulted the days. "March 15, Saturday 8:30 meeting with the Commerce Secretary, then Advisory Committee on Governmental Organization at 8:45, then off to the Statler Hotel for your speech to the AMA, and 11:55 with Colonel Carroll, nothing in the afternoon. Nothing planned for Sunday."

The President rubbed his chin. "Get Ed Baughman and tell him I want to drive up to Gettysburg. Freeze my calendar for Saturday night and Sunday."

"Yes, Mister President."

Edmund Baughman was appointed Secret Service Chief when his predecessor was fired by Truman. The reason was that he dispatched Secret Service agents to New York to guard Thomas E. Dewey, who was expected to win the election but didn't.

He didn't like Truman, or his constantly irritated wife or sourpuss mother-in-law. Ike was different. He listened to and accepted advice from the Secret Service Protective Detail. Ike, unlike Truman, didn't fancy an early morning walk on a public street, a Truman habit that continually vexed the protective detail. But Baughman and his agents weren't there to like or dislike presidents, just protect them.

Ed Baughman hung up the phone and called in his deputy. "Glenn, Scorecard wants to take a trip to Gettysburg."

"Yes sir, when?"

"Saturday afternoon and Sunday. Pick four men, and make it a two-car detail. We don't want to advertise with a convoy. Call over to the White House garage and tell them to get the Lincoln ready. Make sure the cars are checked and gassed up and have radios. Call up to the state police barracks and tell them to sweep the farm and roads. No surprises."

"Yes sir, I'll get right on it. Can I add the new agent to the detail, Roger Bremer?"

"Did his clearance come through?"

"Yes sir, yesterday. Very impressive. Law degree, served with the MPs in Korea.

Top marks in his academy class."

"Okay, Glenn, put him on. Give him a head's up on the president's dos and don'ts."

Special Treasury Agent Roger Bremer was seated in the deputy director's office wondering if he did something wrong.

"Okay, Bremer looks like we got something for you. The president is taking a little trip this weekend and you're on the detail."

"Yes, sir. Where is he going?"

"His farm in Gettysburg. Ever been to Gettysburg?"

"No, sir. I'm from California. Never made it to the east except for basic training."

"The president and first lady own a farm up there. The place is a dump but it's a nice piece of property near the battlefield. They bought it in 1950 and started to fix it up. It's his thinking place. When he was elected we put in security. He won't allow us to fence in the property. Says the battlefield belongs to the people."

"How long will he be there?"

"Not long. Saturday afternoon and Sunday, so basically it's an overnighter. The detail has four agents and two cars. The president will be in the Lincoln Cosmopolitan with a driver and agent. He loves that car. Says it's like sitting in his living room. The Packard will be the support car. You'll ride shotgun upfront. Presidential code name is Scorecard. The man loves his golf. Never broadcast his name or title when in transit. He smokes like a chimney so make sure the ashtray is cleaned out before, during, and after the trip. You're there for his protection. Follow the protocols, speak when spoken to, and stay in the background. Duration of the trip is a couple of hours. Once you're out of the district you get into country roads. Then we have to watch out for deer attacks."

"Sir?"

"Deer attacks, damn things come out of nowhere jumping in front of the car. Agents did this trip last month and a couple of deer came leaping out of the woods. Before you knew it, they were blasting away thinking it was the real deal. Scorecard told them not to shoot. It wasn't deer season."

"Any stops along the way? Bathroom breaks?"

"No, Scorecard doesn't stop, not even for a bathroom break. Oh, he does have a standing rule. If there is a serviceman on the road hitchhiking, he will tell the detail to pick him up. So that's about it. The rest you can ask the agent in charge. Welcome to the Presidential Protective Detail."

At three o'clock Car One and Car Two were waiting at

the rear entrance to the White House. The Lincoln Cosmopolitan four-door sedan, designated Car One, would carry the President, a driver, and one Secret Service agent. Car Two was a standard government Packard. Each car had a two-way radio. Car Two carried a small arsenal of weapons, a standard first aid kit, blankets, water, and a tool kit. Riding in Car Two would be four agents.

By three thirty they realized that the President was running behind schedule. At five o'clock a White House staff member announced that the President would be down in twenty minutes.

Agent Dick Laffler checked his watch for the fifth time. "We're going to be traveling in the dark if we don't get a move on."

"Not our call, Dick. We serve at the pleasure of the President," remarked Agent

Belmont. "Start the cars and get them warmed up."

Belmont motion to Bremer. "Bremer, you ride in Two up front. There's a map in the glove compartment. Familiarize yourself with the route. It gets tricky once we get into Pennsylvania."

At 5:50 President Eisenhower emerged from the residence, cigarette in one hand and a small briefcase in the other. "Okay boys, sorry to keep you waiting. Let's go."

Saturday afternoon traffic was light and easy, and the two cars made good time out of Washington. The sky was clear and the temperature felt like spring was on the way, a good day to take a drive. The President took no notice of the passing scenery as he studied the reports from his briefcase.

By seven o'clock they crossed over into Pennsylvania and the clouds began to close in around the mountains. A light mist spotted the windshields and wisps of fog rolled in the low meadows. The wipers made occasional passes to clear away the wet film, and both cars turned on their headlights.

The President leaned forward. "Can we get some heat back here? It feels like England. Damn cold seeps into your bones."

As they passed into the Catoctin Mountain area visibility was down to the road directly in front of the cars. The lead car carrying the President slowed to thirty and then twenty miles an hour.

Agent Belmont leaned over to the driver. "Nice and easy, we don't want to go off in the ditch."

The town of Thurmont slid past on the right and soon they were alone in the mist.

Belmont used the side mirror to check that the support car was behind them.

"Mr. President, we are just about to cross over to Pennsylvania, won't be long now."

Eisenhower nodded as he lit a cigarette.

In Car Two Agent Laffler was having trouble keeping up. He kept goosing the gas pedal, but the car was losing acceleration. A scan of the dashboard indicated all the dials were in the right place, but the car was slowing down.

"Boys, we got a problem. Something's wrong. Radio the lead car and tell them I'm pulling over."

Bremer reached for the radio. "Car One, this is Car Two. We have a mechanical problem and are pulling over."

Both cars pulled to the side of the road. Laffler had enough power to slide the car to the side of the road. Once it came to a rest the headlights dimmed and then went out. Inside the car Bremer resisted the urge to say anything. The backseat agents got out of the car and surveyed the area around the car. A wall of darkness enveloped the road; the only sound was the clicking of the engine as it cooled.

The Lincoln Cosmopolitan idled twenty feet from the Packard. Senior Agent Belmont noted the time and turned.

"Mr. President, I'm going to check on the other car. Please remain here with the other agents." Ike nodded and settled into the seat.

Belmont walked to the Packard's driver side.

"What's the problem, Dick?"

Laffler tried the ignition once more. Nothing. "It started to lose power, I gave it the gas and it just gave up on me. Now I have nothing, not even a click from the battery."

"Can you fix it?"

"Vern, I don't even know what's wrong with it. We're dead in the water."

"Ok, hand me a flashlight."

Belmont moved to the front of the car and lifted the hood. A puff of smoke trailed out and the area was filled with the smell of rotten eggs. The yellow beam from the flashlight revealed no immediate cause for the breakdown. By now all four agents were in front of the Packard with Belmont.

"We can't stay here. We need to get Scorecard to a secure location. Dick, you and Coyle stay with the car. Wilson, you hike back down the road, find a house, and call headquarters that you need a tow and another car. Carl, when you're on the move radio us and hightail it to Gettysburg. Bremer, you and I will take Scorecard to the farm. Any questions?"

Belmont and Bremer got in and closed the doors on the Lincoln. Belmont turned to the President.

"Mr. President, the support car is out of commission. We are going to proceed to Gettysburg. This is Agent Bremer, one of our best agents."

Bremer could have sworn he saw Belmont wink in the glow of the dashboard light.

Eisenhower clicked on the small work light in the back seat and opened a file. "Alright Vern, let's get moving."

Belmont eased the Lincoln onto the road and in the rear view mirror watched the Packard disappear into the fog.

The road flattened out and the fog lightened enough so that the outlines of trees on both sides were visible. Belmont used the wipers every now and then to clean away the drizzle. Neither agent spoke and the sound from the back seat was the turning of pages.

The fog crawled back as they came upon a farm field. Belmont cautiously slowed the Lincoln. Bremer leaned forward. Belmont glanced over. "Whadda got, Roger?"

Bremer scanned the front again.

"Up ahead, someone's walking in the road. Looks . . . looks like a soldier."

The voice from the back came through loud and clear. "Pick him up."

Belmont looked in the rear view mirror. "Sir, I'd advise against that."

"Come on, Vern. It's a soldier walking in the rain. Remember what that felt like?"

"Yes, sir."

"Roger, I'll pull alongside and you check him out."

The Cosmopolitan slowed and Bremer rolled down the window. "Hey, soldier."

The young man stopped and faced the car. "Yes, sir?"

Bremer looked at the soldier. His winter issue greatcoat was sodden and his green garrison cap was plastered to his head. A sad, tired face stared back at Bremer.

"How about a ride?"

The soldier nodded. "I'd appreciate that sir. Mighty damp out tonight."

Belmont leaned over and told Bremer to get out and put the soldier in the front seat.

"No, Vern, put him back here with me. Put his coat in the trunk and get a blanket."

Belmont knew he was outvoted on this one. The commander-in-chief had his soft spot for a dogface. Bremer got out of the car and opened the trunk. He took the coat and handed the soldier a wool blanket. "Mind your manners."

Bremer opened the back door and the soldier got in.

"Where are you going, soldier?"

It took but a second for the recognition to set in.

"General Eisenhower."

"Actually I got a new title."

"Sorry, sir. Mister President."

Eisenhower turned on the work light. "Let's see. Corporal... What's your name son?"

"Egan sir, Corporal Sam Egan, Dog Company, Third Battalion, Fifteenth Regiment, Third Division. Can Do, Sir."

Eisenhower chuckled "Yes, can do, and where are you walking to Corporal?

"Gettysburg, sir, I'm going home."

Eisenhower smiled. "Me too. Vern, let's get this young man home."

A fast run to Gettysburg was now out of the question. The fog had once more wrapped itself around the presidential car, the headlights useless as the grayness blanked the beams to a few feet. Meanwhile, the two soldiers continued to talk in the back seat.

"Your family owns a farm, Corporal?"

"Yes sir, been there since before Lee came to town. I was driving a tractor before I could get a license. Boys back in basic training grumbled about getting up so early. I told them it was nice to sleep in."

"Where did you do your basic?"

"Believe it or not sir, Indiantown Gap. Didn't have to leave the state."

"That's the army for you, full of surprises."

"Yes sir, the big surprises came later. Seattle to Yokohama to Korea. One thing about the army is that they don't give you time to settle in any one place. After some orientation time in the rear we were trucked up to the MLR. They divided the new guys up and put them with the old timers. Rule number one: don't talk, just listen."

"The value of good NCOs is to teach your men to stay alive."

"Yes sir. Sergeant Waters was the best. Kept my mistakes to a minimum, but didn't let me forget it. Pretty soon I thought my middle name was 'damn fool.'"

Eisenhower smiled. "I know that feeling son. How long were you on the line?"

"A lifetime sir, I didn't know that one little country could have the hottest summers or the coldest winters. Flies big as mice, mosquitoes were full-time blood suckers. Can't forget about the mud. They called it rain, more like a fire hose, after the mud grabbed onto your boots and wouldn't let go."

The President folded his arms "How long were you in the country?"

Egan let out a long breath "Feels like I'm still there sir, long time. You know, minutes seem like hours, hours seem like days. On the line it was two hours on watch, two hours trying to sleep. Night patrols were the worst, past our lines down into the valley, listening for anything that moved. One time we were out crossing this swamp, and half way through this blue mist comes up and starts swirling and wrapping around your legs. The Koreans called it *hon bul,* ghost flames. Said it was spirits of the dead come to claim you. Boys in the company said it showed your number was up." Egan gave a shudder.

Eisenhower leaned over and examined the soldier's jacket. "CIB, Bronze Star with Combat V, Purple Heart... I'd say you gave a good account of yourself."

Egan shook his head. "No sir, just didn't show how scared I was. You know what got to me the most? Silence. At night, in a listening post, when the insects stop and the wind dies down... silence. And then the North Koreans would start blowing those bugles, banging pots, and screaming. You knew what was coming next. Thousands running toward you. Then they're in the front, the sides, and in back of you."

"I'm sorry son. Sorry."

Egan looked at the President. "You don't have to be sorry, sir. I went heads up and knowing things could turn out badly. Looking at those Koreans after the Commies got through with a village . . . . Something needed to be done. You can reason with reasonable people, but those people up North, they're far from reasonable. My only regret is that good men died fighting unreasonable people. A buddy of mine, Jack Colby . . . . We went through basic together. Spent time on leave. He got it after a mortar attack. I held onto him and the last thing he said was 'don't let me go' and then it was over."

Eisenhower replied, "Men in conference rooms make decisions that send good young men like you and your buddy in harm's way. I prayed to God that those who suffered did not do so in vain. Sometimes at night, I can see the faces of the men I sent to Normandy. You've done your country a great service, and it seems all we can do is say thank you."

"I appreciate that Mr. President, but there is something else my sergeant would say. You die twice, once when they put you in the ground, and then when the last person says your name. This country has to learn to remember the ones who never lived to see what the future holds."

"Well said, Corporal, well said."

"The hard part sir, was promising my mom I'd come home. I mean how can you promise something like that? The last time was the worst. We were on a hill, no name, just a number: Hill 182. Snowed off and on all day, so cold I couldn't feel my toes. Then that night they zeroed in with mortars and star shells. The ground exploded around us. One minute I was holding onto the wall of the trench and the next I'm flying through the air. Took forever to land, and when I did I didn't feel anything. . . ."

Agent Laffler turned to the president. "Sir, we're in Gettysburg, where should we drop off the Corporal?"

Egan looked out the window. The fog had thinned and the walls to the National Cemetery were visible. "Here is fine, sir."

Laffler pulled the car over to the shoulder.

Eisenhower looked around. "Son, it's no problem to drop you at your house."

Egan opened the door "No sir, this is fine. Thank you for the ride, and sorry for talking so much. Most I've done in a long time."

Eisenhower leaned over and extended his hand. "One soldier to another, I enjoyed our time. Good luck, son."

Egan gripped the president's hand. It was cold as ice. "Thank you, sir. Goodbye."

Egan put on his campaign hat and closed the door. Laffler pulled onto the road and headed toward the Eisenhower farm.

Bremer turned his head and looked at the president. "Mr. President, he forgot his coat."

Eisenhower lit a cigarette. "No problem, you can swing by his house tomorrow and drop it off."

The men were quiet as the car made its way down the one-mile road to the farmhouse. Laffler swung the car around the turnaround. "Mr. President, just let us do a look around."

Once inside Ike made his way to his desk and picked up his notebook and then went upstairs. He felt tired from his trip and retired for the night.

Rising early the next day, the President dressed and went downstairs. Laffler had already prepared a pot of coffee. "Good Morning, Mr. President."

"Morning, Vern. Looks like a beautiful day."

"Yes sir. Big difference from last night."

"Oh, speaking of that, how about getting that coat to Corporal Egan?"

"I sent Bremer to his house sir, should be back anytime. Coffee Mr. President?"

"Good, good. I'll take a cup at my desk."

Eisenhower lit his traditional breakfast cigarette and settled into his desk chair. The contents of his briefcase were spread out on the desk. He was glad he had made the trip to recover his notebook. He liked—no. He loved Gettysburg, and the blissful quiet of the Pennsylvania countryside.

Engrossed in his work the president did not notice that Laffler and Bremer were standing in the doorway.

"Got my coffee, Vern?"

"Sir, there's something you should hear from Agent Bremer."

"Sure, what is it?"

Bremer took a step toward the president. "Mr. President, I went to the Egan place and spoke to Mrs. Egan. Well, sir. . . . She... I think you should read this, sir."

Bremer handed the President a copy of the *Gettysburg Times*. Eisenhower put on his glasses.

"Bremer, what am I looking at?"

"It's Friday's edition, sir. Lower left on the front page."

Eisenhower turned the paper.

Local Hero Laid To Rest

The body of Corporal Samuel Egan, son of Charlotte and Benjamin Egan, was buried Thursday at the National Soldiers Cemetery. Corporal Egan was killed during an Communist attack on his position at Hill 182 near Jeokbin-Ri, Korea. The parents were notified of his death in February, and the body was sent home last week. Corporal Egan was awarded the Bronze Star with V, the Purple Heart, and the National Defense Medal. Internment will take place on Thursday after a service at the...

"My God," said the president.

"Sir, I'm sure it was somebody pretending to be Corporal Egan. I mean the only possible explanation—" began Laffler.

Eisenhower held up his hand. "Why don't you give me a minute to think this over. In the meantime, get the car ready."

Both agents nodded and walked away.

Ike laid the paper down. Could it be possible, or was it just a terrible joke?

"Mr. President, the car is out front."

It was a short drive to the National Soldier's Cemetery. Laffler pulled over to the entrance on Taneytown Road. Bremer got out and opened the rear door. The President got out, and placed his hat on his head.

"I want you to wait here. There is something I have to do."

Eisenhower walked past the wrought iron gate at the entrance and looked at the row upon row of headstones.

The cool breeze stirred the boughs of the trees. It was as if nature was whispering to him. He started to walk down the left walkway, drawn by a feeling guiding him on. As he walked he read the headstones: Belleau Woods, Argonne Forest, Normandy, Saipan, Okinawa, North Africa.

In an open space he saw a fresh grave and a wreath of flowers resting on the white marble. Ike walked to the grave and took off his hat. He moved the wreath and read the inscription.

Samuel John Egan, Pennsylvania, Corporal, D Company, 15th Regiment, 3rd Battalion, U.S. Army, Korea, July 2, 1931 - February 5, 1953.

President Eisenhower placed his hand on the headstone.

"I'm glad you made it home, Sam. You and so many like you answered when your country called. You didn't go to Korea on your own. We sent you. You went and fought, and died because you believed in your country and its cause. But I'm going to promise you here, now, I will not send other young men into harm's way without cause or reason that protect this country. Rest now Sam. I won't forget you."

Ike felt a small flutter in his chest and took a deep breath. He turned and started to walk back. The stillness of this sacred place made him feel at peace. In the distance he could see the two Secret Service agents, ever watchful. Bremer moved to meet the president.

"Everything alright, sir?"

"Yes, Agent Bremer. Everything is alright. Now, time to get back to Washington and back to work."

Bob Scappini is an educator, historian, and writer. His first novel, *Fire Across the Sky* is a period thriller with Thomas Edison. In his spare time he reconstructs historic walls for the National Park Service.

The Circle of Death

By James Rada Jr.

Hector Diaz walked down the row of apple trees in Jake Planchette's orchard, carrying a couple of empty bushel baskets stacked within each other. He looked at tree after tree that workers had picked clean of fruit as he searched for his starting place for the day's work.

He saw the tall tree heavy with red apples and dropped the baskets. Then he screamed and made the sign of the cross in front of himself.

The Pennsylvania State Police arrived a short time later. Usually, most of the workers would have vanished at the sight of law enforcement. They didn't want to be asked about their immigration status. Although nearly all of them were in the country legally on work visas, they preferred not to have to deal with the police at all.

Trooper Derek Johnson had to park in the grass just off PA-34 north of Biglerville and walk back to where the body was located because there wasn't enough room between the rows of apple trees, and a police vehicle or pick-up truck filled any spot closer. He could easily see where he was going because of the crowd gathered around a tree about a quarter mile from the road.

"What do we got?" he asked as he reached the group.

Trooper Pete Weikert turned and shrugged. "You tell me because I would sure like to know."

Derek wrinkled his brow at the cryptic answer. Then he moved in closer. The call had said a body had been found beneath a tree in the orchard.

That might have been a generous description.

The word body inferred that it had flesh. This one didn't. It was a skeleton wearing a set of clothes. Derek couldn't see any marks of foul play, but then the best he might hope to see were broken bones. There weren't any. All he could see were what looked like tree roots coming out of the ground and between the bones. However, those roots were thick, indicating they had been growing for years, which meant the body had been there for years.

"When did they dig him up?" Derek asked.

Pete shook his head. "They didn't. He was like that this morning."

Derek stared at the body. "Then someone would have reported this months ago. It takes time for a body to become a skeleton and roots to grow up through it."

"That's the thing, Derek. This body wasn't here yesterday. These workers were picking fruit here yesterday and would have seen it. No one did."

Derek pointed at the body. "Then they're lying. Look at it. It's been here a long time."

"Why would they lie about not seeing it yesterday, but report it today?"

Derek shook his head. It made no sense.

The EMTs approached, carrying their ambulance stretcher, which was easier than trying to push the wheeled one over the rough ground. The man and woman stopped when they saw the body.

"Uh, what are we supposed to do with that?" the man asked. "That's not a body."

"Plus, it's tangled in those roots," the female EMT said.

Derek started walking back to his car. He passed the county coroner on his way to the skeleton.

"Where are you going?" Dr. Wilkinson asked.

"I've got a hatchet in my trunk," Derek told him.

"Hatchet? What do you need a hatchet for?"

"You'll see."

Derek opened the trunk of his car and moved equipment around until he found a hatchet he kept for emergencies. Then he walked back to the tree and chopped through the roots. It wasn't easy. At times, they felt like iron, and at other times, rubber. The skeleton still had much of its connective tissue, so the EMTs could lift most of it in one piece onto the gurney.

The EMTs carried the skeleton to their ambulance. They transported it to the morgue at Gettysburg Hospital where Dr. Wilkinson would examine it later. Once the police and EMTs were gone, Jake Planchette walked through the crowd of his workers, saying, "Okay, you had your CSI for today. It's time to get back to work."

The group of men and women separated, heading off to where trees were full of fruit. Jake noticed that none of them moved to pick the apples from the heavily laden tree where the body had been found.

Nor did they ever pick the fruit. The tree remained unpicked and untended. The fruit and leaves should have dropped off in the fall. They remained, though, even when the surrounding trees were barren. The snows fell, and the tree stood in the orchard, a lone sentinel of the murder and death that had taken place.

The body was never identified, and no one claimed it. Dr. Wilkinson kept a small bone should he or the police need it for identification. He cremated the rest of the skeleton, and the ashes were spread over a field.

Someone tried to cut the deadly apple tree down one spring night. The chainsaw they used apparently couldn't make it all the way through the trunk. People found a large notch cut from the tree, but it continued standing, and within a week, the notch had filled in. Only now, the new bark was red like the skin on the apples. People said it reminded them of the Joker's grin from the Batman comics.

One night, someone set the tree on fire. The Biglerville Fire Company showed up, but no one rushed to put out the fire. They were happy to see the tree burn. The firefighters simply made sure the flames didn't spread to the rest of the orchard.

When the flames died off, all that was left was a blackened trunk and the thicker branches. Satisfied, the firefighters returned home. The next morning, the apples had regrown, plump and red, only now they reminded people of pus-filled sores ready to burst. The bark remained blackened, except for the Joker's smile. Despite burning, that section of bark turned red again, mocking with its silent laughter.

Someone tried poisoning the tree, spreading an herbicide around the trunk. No one noticed any change in the tree. It was the surrounding ground that turned dead. Grass within eight feet of the tree died. No animals crawled through the dirt. The black tree with the blood drops hanging from its branches and the Joker's smile suddenly found itself an oasis in a dead zone of ground.

People got the message. They left the tree alone. They called it "the laughing demon" and said its fruit, the demon seed, was deadly to any who ate it. Not that anyone put that particular legend to the test. It was the only tree in the orchard never harvested. Workers hated even having to spend time near it.

***

Jenny Hoechlin stared at the laughing demon. She knew her next step would bring her within the dead zone, within its realm. From the tree to a point eight feet from the trunk, the ground was dead and gray dirt, yet somehow the tree survived, although it looked as if it should be dead itself.

She saw the blood-drop apples hanging from the branches, looking like they were ready to fall.

Would this work? She knew the stories. They were probably just that, but her husband, Kyle, was always so cautious, so suspicious of her. She needed to do something he wouldn't expect. She needed something impossible.

Jenny stepped across the line.

Nothing happened.

She wasn't sure what she had expected. Maybe to be struck dead like everything else inside the line. What was she thinking? She didn't want to die, but she was tired of Kyle hitting her, tired of the suspicion, tired of the lies.

Jenny reached up and plucked four apples from the black branches. They felt oily, as if they would slip from her fingers. She dropped them into a bag she had brought with her.

She drove home to the apartment she and Kyle shared above Food 101 on Chambersburg Street in Gettysburg. She peeled and sliced the apples and baked them into a pie. Apple pie was Kyle's favorite. He came home around 5:30 p.m. from his job walking around town writing parking tickets for the borough.

She watched him sniff at the air. "Is that apple pie?" he asked.

"Yes, I took it out of the oven a couple of minutes ago."

He turned and squinted. "What did you do?"

Jenny smiled and prayed she didn't look guilty. "What do you mean?"

"You making me a pie must be because you did something wrong."

Jenny shook her head. "I didn't. I promise. I just wanted to do something nice for you."

Kyle's eyes narrowed even more. "Uh-huh."

He walked into the kitchen and saw the pie cooling on the counter. He inhaled deeply and then looked at Jenny. He pulled a knife from a drawer, and Jenny flinched. He ignored her reaction and cut a slice of pie and slid it onto a small plate. Jenny was tempted to tell him to wait until after dinner, but she wanted him to eat the pie.

Kyle took the pie to the table and sat down. Jenny held her breath as he took a bite.

He smiled. Then he took another bite.

Jenny's knees went weak. She kept herself from falling by leaning against the counter.

Kyle finished his slice and held out the plate to Jenny. "Give me another slice."

Jenny took the plate, cut another slice, and handed him the plate. It might not have killed him, but at least he was happy. She should be safe. For tonight, at least.

The pie put Kyle in a good mood. He ate dinner without complaint. He didn't yell at her, although he didn't compliment her either. Things hadn't worked out how she had hoped, but they had worked out.

Jenny awoke in the morning before her husband. She had to make sure she had breakfast ready by the time he got up for work. She went into the kitchen and saw the pie. She was tempted to throw it out, since it hadn't ended her problem. It had only placated Kyle and given Jenny an evening of peace. However, if she threw the pie away, it would only anger Kyle because he had enjoyed it so much.

She scrambled eggs and fried bacon. She set it on a plate with buttered toast. Then she realized she hadn't heard Kyle stirring.

"Kyle, breakfast is ready," she called.

No answer.

She walked to the door of the bedroom. Kyle lay on the bed with his eyes open.

"Kyle, breakfast is on the table." He didn't stir. "Kyle?"

She walked into the bedroom and shook him by the shoulder. He didn't move. Her hand began shaking. She touched her fingers to his neck, and she didn't feel a pulse.

She stepped back.

Had it worked?

She pulled her smartphone from her pocket and called 911. When the operator answered, Jenny said, "I think my husband's dead."

Dr. John Wilkinson looked at the body on the metal table in the morgue at Gettysburg Hospital. He turned on the recorder.

"This is Adams County Coroner John Wilkinson performing the autopsy of Kyle Hoechlin. He died in his sleep with no apparent cause. The body shows no signs of trauma. No bruising or wounds. I will test his blood for toxins and poisons."

He picked up a syringe and inserted it into a vein on the body's arm. As he pulled the plunger back, no blood flowed into the tube. He withdrew the needle and checked the arm to find another spot to withdraw blood. It was not easy since there was no blood pressure. He tapped at the corpse's arm and pressed into the skin. He finally found a vein. It felt solid. He inserted the needle, but again, he couldn't draw any blood.

Frowning, John picked up a scalpel from the tray and sliced open the vein in the arm. He did not find pooling blood as he had expected but a red sludge that was the consistency of pudding. As he watched, it oozed out of the vein, although it was not being pumped out by a beating heart. John used the scalpel blade to scrape some of the sludge out and drop it into an empty test tube. He wasn't sure if this thick blood was the cause or effect of Hoechlin's death. It was unlike anything he had seen and certainly nothing he had expected.

He capped the tube and placed it in the cooler. Then he proceeded to open up Hoechlin's body and began his internal examination.

***

Carl Pitzer placed a drop of the blood sample onto a slide, covered it, and placed it under the microscope. He put his eye to the eyepiece and focused on the sample. The automated test results had come back inconclusive. Carl had never had that happen. The only thing he could think of was the sample was contaminated . . . very contaminated, but Dr. Wilkinson had verified he had drawn the blood directly from the patient with a blood collection tube.

He squinted, drew back, and rubbed his eyes. The cells were red with nuclei and other cellular structures. However, they were squarish and compacted against each other like plant cells, but animal cells didn't have cell walls and chloroplasts.

He called over to a nearby medical technologist. "Tina, take a look at this."

"What is it?"

"It is supposed to be a blood sample."

"Supposed to be?"

"Take a look."

Tina Hammond bent over the microscope and adjusted the eyepiece. Carl picked up the test tube and stared at it. He tilted it to the side. It moved reluctantly like thick syrup.

"If I had to classify it as something, I would say it's blood."

"Animal or human?"

Tina frowned and sucked on his lower lip. "Plant? Don't laugh," she added quickly.

"I'm not. I thought the same thing."

"How are you going to write up the results?"

Carl held up the vial and stared at it. It looked like blood, but it did not move like blood. It moved like . . . slow-creeping lava. But lava wasn't red or cool. This was neither. This was both. It had a beauty in the way it undulated like oil and water in a kid's toy, but it held onto its mystery of what it was.

He felt a hand on his shoulder as it shook him.

"Carl. Carl?"

Carl blinked and turned to Tina. "What?"

"What were you thinking? You zoned out on me."

"I heard you. You just asked how I am going to write up the results. I don't know."

"That was like two minutes ago. I said you should get the pathologist to look at this. Then I looked over, and you were all glassy eyed, staring at the vial."

Carl glanced at it and then looked away quickly in case he got . . . lost in it again.

He set the test tube in the rack and picked up a pen to make notes.

He squinted in the bright sunlight. He raised a hand to cover his eyes and saw that he was holding an empty test tube.

What?

He looked around. How did he get outside? He had been in the hospital laboratory. He'd been getting started writing up the results of the blood test.

Then what happened?

He couldn't remember. How could he not remember leaving work? He wasn't asleep, so he couldn't have been sleepwalking.

And why did he have an empty test tube? He looked at it. Empty, but used. It had a bit of residue in it. Carl looked at the label. It was Dr. Wilkinson's odd sample.

His hand shook. That sample! There was something about that sample that was wrong. Tina had said Carl had zoned out looking at it. Had something like that happened again? No, he hadn't zoned out this time. He had walked out of the lab, through hallways, making turns in the labyrinth of passages, and left the building. All without . . . what? Being awake? Remembering?

He dropped the vial. Gettysburg had its odd happenings. The city had turned ghost stories into a cottage industry. This was far creepier.

He looked around and got his bearings. He hurried across the parking lot to his car. He hesitated, unsure whether he should drive. He didn't want to black out again and get in an accident. If he was going to black out again, he wanted to know the reason why.

He drove across South Washington Street to the alley behind Dobbin House Tavern. He went through the parking lot to Steinwehr and then through the parking lot for the Inn at Cemetery Hill to get to Baltimore Street and the parking lot behind O'Rorke's Restaurant. He went inside and started downing beers. At some point during the evening, he called off work for a week, but although he was good and drunk, he still remembered it the next morning, unlike when he had been near the blood sample.

***

Jared Heffner saw the small bush with red leaves while he was cutting the lawn at Gettysburg Hospital the next day. Since he did all the landscaping for the hospital, he knew it hadn't been there yesterday. He kept track of things like that.

He turned off the lawnmower and knelt down next to the bush. He didn't recognize the species. He saw something shiny poking from underneath the bush. He picked it up and saw it was an empty vial.

He yelped as a leaf sliced him across the back of the hand. Blood seeped out of the cut. He lifted his hand and saw that the cut wasn't deep. How had it happened, though? The bush didn't have thorns. Were the leaves that sharp?

He stared at the bush, then back at his hand. He felt his blood pumping, although nothing seemed to come from the wound. He looked at the bush but still saw nothing that would cut him.

He reached down, his hand hovering over the bush. He felt a thrumming, as if electricity was running through the bush. Suddenly, blood ran from the wound in his hand. Three drops rolled between his fingers and dropped onto the bush. The bush actually trembled. The blood faded into the leaves as if the leaves had absorbed it.

Then Jared felt something run through his body. He stiffened, and his eyes turned glassy.

He put his hands on either side of the bush and lifted it up. It came free of the ground easily, as if it didn't even have roots.

He stood up and walked away from the hospital to his truck, which was parked in a corner of the parking lot. He opened the passenger door and set the bush on the seat. Then he walked around and climbed into the driver's seat.

He drove north out of Gettysburg and beyond Biglerville. He turned off Route 34 and into one of the many orchards in this area of Gettysburg. He parked the pickup truck and carried the bush with him as he walked further into the orchard.

He stopped at the edge of the dead circle around the black tree, barren except for the blood-drop apples.

He hesitated at the edge of the circle. Then he stepped across the invisible line and walked to the tree. He set the bush next to the trunk of the tree. The bush with red leaves shriveled up and seemed to melt into the ground.

Jared laid down next to the tree and closed his eyes. A root shot up from the ground. It plunged into his back and out of his chest. Jared's eyes flared open. He gasped, but he did not scream. His hands clenched and then relaxed.

***

Trooper Derek Johnson parked his cruiser and hiked back into the orchard. How long had it been since he had last been here? Two years?

He froze when he saw the body. It looked nearly the same as the body had when Derek had been here the last time.

"What is this?" he asked Pete Weikert who had also been on the call two years ago.

Pete shook his head. "I know. It looks almost the same, but I don't know how."

"The tree is different."

"No, it's the same one. It just looks different. People have tried to get rid of it, but nothing works."

Derek pointed at the body. "That can't be the same. We took the other body away."

Pete shrugged. "Like I said. It looks the same, but I don't know how it could be. We don't even know what happened to the other body."

Derek sighed. "Any ID on the body?"

"We found a truck owned by Jared Heffner near here. We've tried to get a hold of him, but haven't had any luck."

"You think this is him?"

The other trooper shrugged. "I don't know how it could be. People saw him at work yesterday, but it's a lead."

"Where does he work?"

"Gettysburg Hospital."

So why would a hospital employee drive out here, leave his truck, and . . . then what? Turn into a skeleton impaled by a tree?"

"So, if we take this body, how long do you think it will be before we come back here and find another skeleton?"

The other trooper shrugged. "Circle of life, I guess."

Derek glanced at the body and shuddered. "More like a circle of death."

James Rada, Jr. is an Amazon.com bestselling author who writes historical fiction and non-fiction history. His books include *Saving Shallmar: Christmas Spirit in a Coal Town, Canawlers,* and *Battlefield Angels: The Daughters of Charity Work as Civil War Nurses*.

James has received awards from the Maryland-Delaware-DC Press Association, Associated Press, Maryland State Teachers Association, Society of Professional Journalists, and Community Newspapers Holdings, Inc. for his newspaper writing.

If you would like to keep up to date on new books James publishes or ask him questions, go to *www.jamesrada.com.*

The Colors of the Storm

By Judith Cameron Seniura

Anna did not just dislike her intended. She despised him.

"My dear," she told her best friend, Ella, "he is simply *odious*." She pronounced the word in her stepmother's nasal British accent, causing the two older women sitting on the divan to look over sharply. One was Margaret, Ella's mother; the other, Laura, Anna's young stepmother.

Ella giggled. "Anna, he cannot be that bad," she murmured. Anna was to marry in summer, an arrangement that would build significant ties for her father in the new industrial center of Toronto in British North America.

"Oh, Ella, but he is. His skin is all mushy, and I don't think he bathes. He's old - at least thirty, and his breath…" She looked heavenward. "Really, I'd rather be downwind of a horse's farting arse."

"Anna!" The coarse language shocked Ella, two years younger than her friend.

"Ladies, what is going on over there?" inquired Margaret, a tall, stately woman who was holding her cup of tea in the latest fashion, pinky out. "Nothing, Mama," said Ella, and bent over her embroidery hoop. She sat upright in her full-skirted dress, her light hair secured to the sides of her head in two buns.

Laura, looking pointedly at Anna through dark, shrew like eyes, asked "Have you put down your needlework? You won't catch a beau with those sloppy stitches."

Anna sighed and picked up her work, which she noted looked far worse than her friend's. Her dark hair was carelessly looped in a loose knot, curls escaping and framing her large brown eyes. But seventeen-year-old Anna could not be bothered with such nonsense. She longed to be out on horseback, hunting with her father and brother as she had for three years after her mother's death. But then Anna's father had married Laura, barely five years her senior and all of Anna's freedom evaporated like the dew on a sweltering summer morning.

Instead of riding unrestrained in the country, hair flying behind her, the sun daring to brown her lily-white skin, her stepmother had thrust Anna into a world of corsets, calligraphy, and domestic crafts. How Anna detested her.

Ella was both awed and appalled by her older friend. At fifteen, she longed to learn how to manage a household so that she might be a better helpmate for whomever she should marry and provide with healthy male heirs.

"Wait until it happens to you," Anna hissed at her blue-eyed companion and sighed. "I wish I were a man. Then, I could do anything -- go out without an escort, sail the seas, and travel the world. What adventures I might have."

"Being a man is dangerous," Ella countered. "Look at how many of them are dying in that awful war in America. Even men from our country have volunteered and never come back."

"Well, yes, but if there were ever a cause to fight for, it

would surely be to free those poor slaves. I would join in the fight if I could." Suddenly, Anna's needle stopped in mid-stitch. She turned to her friend. "Ella, that's brilliant. I could make my way to those American colonies and join up. I'm tall, strong, and can shoot as well as any man." Then she grinned. "And I like to curse."

Ella's eyes opened wide in horror. "Anna, you would not dare. You cannot. Please say you will not leave me. I would worry so much about you. Do not even tease that way."

Anna leaned closer so as not to be overheard. "I'm not teasing. I could sneak out and get on a boat at the harbor, cross over to the Americas and find a regiment to join. It wouldn't be that difficult. I heard Jacob talking about it, and he said several of his companions were thinking of doing just such a thing." She was becoming breathless now in her enthusiasm. "And I'll borrow clothes from Jacob like I did when I was a child. He is not so much larger than I."

As Anna talked increasingly about proceeding with the charade, Ella grew more and more worried. Her friend might do what she said. She could be reckless that way.

"You will never get away with it," whispered Ella. "Someone will notice you are a girl, and everyone will shun you. Your reputation will be ruined!"

Anna grabbed her bottom lip with her teeth in thought. "You may be right," she agreed, "so I'll have to test it. I'll dress up in Jacob's clothes, sneak out of the house one night and take a conveyance down to the harbor. If I can walk around and not be called '*woman*,' I will know I can do it." She turned to Ella, excitement dancing from her eyes. "Ella, come with me."

Ella moved away from her friend. "What? No, Anna, no. I would never… I could never. Look at me. I am half your size, and I am not strong like you. No. This is foolish talk. Anna, please do not do this."

Anna smiled at her. "It will be so much fun," she promised. "I'll find clothes for you at the church poorhouse on Sunday. Then we'll practice. We'll watch the way men walk, converse, and learn to copy them." She grabbed her friend's hands.

"It will be such an adventure, Ella. Our last one together before I..." All the light went out of her eyes, and she added quietly, "... marry that awful man. Please, please, you must do this for me. Everything will be different after I wed. At least we will have this to remember. Please." There were tears in Anna's eyes.

Ella nodded her head up and down without really knowing why, basking in her best friend's admiration and approval as the doubts yipped about her like an untrained pup.

Ella's mother and Anna's stepmother were cousins who visited each other two or three times each week, providing ample opportunity for their charges to develop the plan. And it was great fun, Ella had to admit, as the girls crumpled to the floor in giggles. In hushed tones, they plotted when, where, and how. Anna had included her brother, Jacob, in their scheme. At first, he had said no, he would not be part of such a foolhardy adventure, but after realizing he could not dissuade Anna, Jacob agreed to escort them and keep an eye peeled for trouble. While Anna thought this silly, Ella was glad to have a big brother in the background, and it eased her fears.

When the evening finally arrived, Anna was only four weeks away from her nuptials. Ella noticed her friend's demeanor had become more somber, and she no longer was the carefree person she had always known. It was concerning. A cornered Anna could react in strange and, oft times, dangerous ways.

Ella donned the boys' clothing, feeling slightly naked without her corset, pinned up her long blonde hair, and hid it under a cap. Then, when all was silent, she crept out onto her bedroom balcony, shivering from excitement and dread in equal portions. Soon, the clatter of horse hooves announced Jacob had arrived. After helping her from the second-floor balcony, he installed Ella, now Raymond, beside Anna, now Herbert, in the small carriage. True to his word, after lecturing them all the way, Jacob dropped them off and followed behind in the shadows.

"Isn't this wonderful?" Anna asked, and Ella had to admit the freedom was heady. No one even looked their way. They wandered up and down the wharves, peering into cargo holds and gasping at the size of the boats, which seemed so small from their hilltop homes. They watched passengers board a steamer, the vessel's lights blinking brightly in the darkening sky. As they practiced their swagger, they both laughed aloud. Aloud, thought Ella, not the titter behind a hankie their mothers had reared them on, but honest head-back laughter. It was intoxicating.

"Look, a storm is coming across the lake. We should go back," said Ella. They were sitting on a hill overlooking the harbor. Anna lifted her gaze at the low rumble of thunder, and they watched as the dark clouds swept in, bringing streaks of lightning that turned the sky pink and grey and blue. It was uniquely beautiful.

Two lads were coming their way, arm in arm, singing a shocking sea shanty. Anna and Ella looked at each other and grinned. The young men were staggering slightly and belching openly in the evening air.

"Good evening, lads," the taller one said, sticking out his hand, swaying slightly. "I'm Oswald, and this," he said, laughing as his companion stumbled, "is me wee brother Owen."

Nervously, Anna introduced herself as Herbert and Ella as Raymond. Ella did not dare speak. Her voice could not pass as a man's.

Ella pulled at Anna's sleeve, who was now drinking from a flask and exchanging comments with their new companions. She looked about for Jacob to signal the evening was over, but could not see him anywhere. Ella was beginning to grow wary. Where was Jacob? And then she saw him, crumpled on the ground, moaning, and clutching his head. She had no time to alert her friend as two brawny arms grabbed her, stuffed a dirty rag in her mouth, and threw her over a damp and smelly shoulder. She tried to scream for Jacob, but her voice came out as a muffled grunt. A second ruffian tried to snatch Anna, who was fighting back fiercely, kicking and punching too. But she was no match for her kidnapper. Within minutes, the two young women were pushed down the hill and thrown into a dank-smelling boat. A third brute roughly tied their wrists behind their backs and covered them with putrid burlap sacking. They had never been so frightened.

***

The next few days were never ending travel as the group was pushed from one conveyance into another. Six similarly bound and gagged young men were with them, including Oswald and Owen, the two boys who had been singing the shanty. No one was singing now. Anna wondered what had happened to her brother. Each day, more young men appeared and joined the throng, some voluntarily, some not. But Jacob was not among them. From time to time, the guards would remove their gags and give them mean morsels of bread and stagnant water that tasted like it had been dredged through a horse trough.

On the third night of their captivity, Ella began to cry, but Anna shushed her with a look. "Men don't cry," she whispered. They squeezed together and shivered in the damp night air. Beside them, Oswald and Owen were in earnest conversation.

"We've been taken by crimpers, I'm bound," Oswald said in a slightly accented voice. Suddenly Ella spoke up. "Crimpers?"

Oswald looked up sharply at the high-pitched voice, but responded, "Right. You know, them what kidnaps you and then sells you to a regiment to fight in America's war."

"Do you know what happened to Jacob?" Anna asked. "My brother." she continued. "Tall. Blonde. He was near us when we were taken. El… er, Raymond saw him last lying on the ground behind us."

"Aye, I remember him. One of the night watch was helpin' him to his feet when we was bein' hustled down to the wharf, but I saw no more."

Anna looked around at the strange countryside. "Where are we?" she asked, trying to replace the panic in her voice with indifference.

"Far as I can tell," said Owen, "we been travellin' south. I hear they're takin' us to a battle near to Harrisburg, somewhere in the state of Pennsylvania." He nodded at Anna.

Ella did not speak again. She knew her voice would break, or she would start crying, and was worried about what might happen to her if anyone discovered her true gender. She thought Oswald had figured it out, but hoped he would be discreet. Before anything further could be said, the guards rounded everyone up and forced them down a well-worn dirt road at gunpoint.

Anna felt as if she had been marching for hours when they halted and observed the lead guard speaking with a man in a dark blue uniform. She whispered to Ella, "That's a union soldier." He handed their captor a sack, heavy with the sound of coins, and the kidnappers faded into the forest.

The soldier mounted his horse and rode up and down, prodding captives with his musket. He finally spoke.

"You are in America and have been conscripted into the Union Army." A second soldier began to un-muzzle everyone, although their hands remained bound behind them. "We need every able-bodied man"-- he glanced at Ella, shaking his head at her petite form -- "to help push those bastard rebels back to their stinkin' cotton fields."

"What if we don't want to join no army?" said a surly individual. The soldier sat back in his saddle as if considering the question. "Well, I suppose you could take yer chance with the hunderds of rebs that're in the area or" -- he pointed to where the guards had disappeared -- "with them. But if you stay with us, you get thirteen dollars a month, three meals, and a pension. I doubt you can do better 'n' that whatever tree you fell out of. Now, march ye heathens. March!"

And march they did. Each man received a musket, a uniform, and a bayonet at one point. Ella could hardly carry her gun because it was longer than she was tall and heavy. They were taught how to load it, but she was clumsy. One night, after an arduous day's travel, she simply laid it down and never picked it up again.

Anna was in her glory. She marched with ease and managed the weapon as if it were an old acquaintance. She joked with Oswald and Owen, with whom she had become friends. Although men who had been captured would desert along the way, it was the furthest thing from Anna's mind. She was, however, increasingly worried about her friend. Ella was falling behind and had lost her rifle. She often heard her crying when no one else was nearby. She was pale and sickly looking.

"I want to go home," Ella said the next day. "I'm going to leave."

"No," Anna hissed. "You'll be shot."

Ella shrugged. "Shot now or shot later. I must get away." She paused to wipe the sweat from her brow. "Anna, this is your adventure. It was never meant to be mine. I am no good at soldiering." Tears trickled down her face, unchecked, and then, to Anna's horror, she pulled off her cap and let her blond hair tumble around her shoulders. And cried even harder. Not ladylike sniffs, but great wailing sobs. An officer came over to investigate.

"Well, I'll be damned to Hell," he said, used to addressing men, not young women. "What've we got here?"

***

After Ella was discharged and divested of her uniform, the not-unkindly officer gave her the option of following the army at the rear. She would be with other women who served the army in numerous ways, primarily as cooks and laundresses. Many were wives who had accompanied their husbands into battle. Since Ella did not know where she was or how to get home, she stayed. At least it would give her a chance to be close to Anna and, in time, persuade her to leave this all behind and help Ella find her way back home.

It was near evening when one soldier, weary of marching, stumbled on a large rock and fell, puncturing his upper arm on a sharp piece of shale rock. He lay on the ground, moaning in great pain, while blood streamed from the wound. Ella, hearing his cries, came to his side. She smoothed his brow, gave him a bit of water from a nearby stream, and wrapped the wound in a strip of cloth. He thanked her and said in a low voice, "You are my angel; come down from heaven. Marry me." Ella laughed, saying there was nothing heavenly about her, but later admitted to Anna that she had been proud to assist the man.

Some excitement greeted the column the next day when the group arrived in Hanover, a small town south of Harrisburg. People were waving flags, and tables filled with bits of food and drink filled the streets. There was a large regiment of Union soldiers, newly arrived and the townspeople were giving them a heroes' welcome.

It was July 1, and one of the hottest days Ella had ever known. It might have been a festive scene except for the dead horses in the streets from a recent battle. The stench was truly nauseating. She caught up with Anna in the early evening, and they swatted at the flies that seemed everywhere.

"Anna, what is happening?"

"We are marching into battle in a small town called Gettysburg. The others are talking about it." She pointed to the soldiers. "That's the 16th Michigan Infantry, just arrived from fighting in the south. We're to join them." Anna's eyes glowed with excitement.

"Then we must leave, Anna. We must leave tonight. You cannot go with them. Have you lost your senses? You will be killed. There is death all around us. This is not your war. This is not even your country."

"But it is a cause I believe strongly in, American or not. Just yesterday, I met a man of African descent from Canada East who came all this way to fight for his brothers' freedom, even though he had only crossed over to freedom several months ago. If dying here is my destiny, then so be it." And Anna would not debate it further. The two friends sat quietly together, watching as the sun began its descent in a sweltering sky, filling the evening with deep red, grey, and blue streaks.

"Listen, Ella," Anna said, taking off her hat and grabbing for her boot knife. "I want you to take this, and if anything happens to me..." Anna hacked off a piece of her hair and wrapped it in her handkerchief. She handed it to her distressed friend.

"Anna, I..." her eyes watered and tears spilled over. "I do not want to lose you. You are my best friend. I do not want a locket or a brooch with your hair. Please, do not do this."

Anna took her dear friend's hand and held it, and the two sat silently for a few minutes until a bugle sounded, stopping the low chatter of the men. "We're marching out," said Anna. She hugged her friend fiercely and left. Ella sat stunned, watching as the tired soldiers dragged themselves back to their feet and moved one foot in front of the other to a rhythm of war.

***

At times that night, Anna's mind would sometimes go back to her comfortable home and soft bed. She scratched at her head where the lice had taken root. After giving Ella her lock of hair, Anna had hacked off the rest. It was only ever in the way and now, cropped and shaggy, she smiled at what her fiancé would think if he could see her. Former fiancé, she thought to herself. For whatever happened, Anna would never marry. She knew that now.

The mile-long procession of soldiers moved in step, Anna among hundreds. The mood became muted as they neared their destination, as much from the sober thought of engaging in battle as the fatigue of marching day in and day out.

"Have you seen battle, sir?" she asked one nearby companion.

"We seen nothin' but. We fought at Richmond, Yorktown, and Chancellorsville," he said, spitting out a wad of tobacco. That was a bad 'un. We was run into the ground."

"I've not seen battle yet. But I know how to shoot and defend myself."

The soldier took her measure and shook his head. "Well, that's good cause yer about to get a lot of practice doing that." Afterward, though she questioned him further, he had nothing to say.

Early in the morning, they stopped and, to a man, fell where they had been standing to grab a couple of hours' sleep. Up again at dawn, they continued into the town of Gettysburg, where the mood seemed strangely subdued. There were brief episodes of cannonade and musket fire, but for much of the day, the men marched into formation. It was late afternoon when the fighting began, and confusion soon ensued. The artillery and cannon fire became intense, and everyone was hurrying.

Not long after, an officer appeared on horseback, shouting, waving, and pointing to the top of a hill. Within minutes, her unit was suddenly running up the side of a steep slope. Arriving at its stony peak, they quickly positioned themselves south of the tip of what she learned was called Little Round Top. Her unit took cover behind a great mass of boulders. Anna watched in horror as men and horses screamed and fell, wounded and dead. The profound smell of sweat and blood, cordite and smoke, confusion, and fear permeated the sweltering temperatures. The noise was deafening, and she spat out the taste of dust and metal.

For what seemed like sometimes only a minute and at others, an eternity, Anna spent the rest of the day crouching, loading, standing, and firing. She could tell their unit was flagging. The confederates outnumbered them, and she feared they would all die. And then, thankfully, a second Union regiment came up in support. By now, her ammunition had run out, so she did as she'd seen others do, fixed her bayonet to the end of her musket, and prepared to test her mettle against the enemy in a face-to-face conflict.

One minute she was preparing to join the melee, and the next, Anna's world went silent. She felt her left arm droop, and then all feeling seemed to disappear. She couldn't stand any longer and slowly sank to her knees, then rolled to the side, striking her head on a rock.

When she awoke, the din of war had returned like a great roar of thunder. She glanced down, expecting to see her arm on fire, it pained her so, but it just hung there, flesh mangled, and bone exposed, the sleeve of her uniform missing. Slowly, she reached out her right arm and grabbed a rock to pull herself back up the hill. Someone ran across her body, unaware of whether she was alive, and crushed her back with heavy boots. Still, she continued, inch by bloody inch, passing out and coming to, climbing, and resting until, at last, she leaned against the trunk of an old, gnarled tree. She closed her eyes and tried to regulate her breathing when she began to topple slowly sideways. She was never conscious of hitting the blood-soaked ground.

***

Hours later, Oswald was looking for his brother, Owen. He walked slowly through the dead and wounded, trying to find him. He was thirsty and tired, but he couldn't leave without his brother. The last he had seen him, Owen had been brandishing his bayonet at a rebel soldier. And then he saw him lying at the base of a small hill. Rushing over and crying out his name, Oswald stopped suddenly. The gash across his brother's chest told him Owen was dead. Holding back the tears that threatened to come, he lifted his brother's limp form over his shoulder and carried him to where he had seen a mass grave being dug to bury the many corpses. He said a prayer and crossed himself. Owen would have to lie in peace here, far from his homeland, but a hero to the cause. He lay him down gently and touched his face one last time, before slowly turning to walk away.

Another limp form lay nearby, the arm mangled beyond belief. Oswald shook his head. So much death. But then he paused. Had the soldier's chest risen? Was he breathing? Venturing closer, he knelt. It was his friend Herbert! He felt for a pulse and could feel a quickening beneath his fingertips. Someone grabbed Herbert's feet and began to drag the body toward the edge of the large grave when Oswald shouted for them to stop. "This one's alive. Where is a surgeon?" The fellow shrugged, dropped the soldier's feet, and pointed down across the field.

Oswald picked up his friend and carried him across the field into a medical tent. An aide took one look at the form and called for the surgeon. "Arm," he shouted and proceeded to remove Herbert's shirt, shoving Oswald behind him. The surgeon walked over to assess the body, now nearly naked from the waist up, except where bindings covered the chest.

He shook his head sadly. "Man or woman," he said, "this soldier needs their arm cut off, or they will die."

"Woman?" Oswald asked. "Herbert.?" And then he smiled.

***

While Anna and the 16th Michigan were scrambling up to the peak of Little Round Top, Ella and the rest of the women following were just nearing the town of Gettysburg. One of the supply wagons had broken an axle, and the group stopped to grab some sleep while the repairs were done.

As she gratefully closed her eyes, Ella wondered how her family was faring in Toronto. Did they fear her dead? Was her mother, even now, dressed in black bombazine, refusing to receive visitors? She wished she could send a message to let them know she was safe, or if not safe, at least still alive. But there had been no chance and certainly no paper or ink.

Late the next day as they approached the site of the battle, the sound of fighting became increasingly loud. It soon grew to a crescendo, punctuated by shouts and screams. As they crested a small hill, Ella stared in horror. The noise had become deafening, and bodies were everywhere. She glanced around in a panic, trying to pick out Anna, but it was impossible with thousands of soldiers swarming the fields and hills. She placed her hands over her ears and turned to run away when she felt something grab her ankle. Looking down, she saw that her assailant was a man missing half his face. He was mouthing, 'water,' and without thinking, she ran to the nearest dwelling and asked respectfully for a cup of water for the wounded man.

The woman who answered the door nodded quickly, handed her a cup, pointed to the well, and closed it again. Ella filled it with cool water and went back to where the man lay. He was still, his eyes fixed and the death flies already settling in his flesh. Ella turned to the side, vomited, and then knelt to say a prayer for his soul. She wondered why God had chosen him of all the thousands of young men it could have been. But Ella soon learned that God had his work cut out for him in this senseless war.

She returned the cup to the farmhouse and reported the soldier was dead. The woman invited her in and gave her a mug of tea and a biscuit, which Ella consumed eagerly. As she took the last sip of the warm liquid, her hostess went to the back kitchen door and hollered out, "Isaac, we got us another 'un." Moments later, a man weathered by farming joined them and asked Ella to show him where the body lay. He pulled a hand cart behind him. When they reached the corpse, he directed her to pick up the young man's feet and help get him up on the cart. Then, they returned to the farm.

His wife greeted them with a wash-pan of water and some rags. After her husband returned to the barn, she said, "Well, come on, girl. This lad ain't gonna bury hisself." They stripped and washed the body, and then Ella helped the older woman wrap it in old sacking. Isaac returned and placed the remains back in the cart, and the small funeral cortege traveled to an open field, where they quickly interred the poor boy. It was the first such event Ella had ever witnessed, but in the coming weeks, there would be hundreds, thousands more, and many treated with far less respect than she and her hosts had given this young soldier.

Ella thanked them for their hospitality and turned to leave when the woman stopped her. "You have a strong heart and a good touch, which plenty are going to need in the next days. Why don't you lend a hand if you've a mind? Spangler's farm is just north of here. They were settin' up a hospital there yesterday, I was told."

She gave Ella the directions and bid her farewell. Ella walked in a north-easterly direction, drawn by a feeling that she, too, was marching to her destiny. Occasionally, a cannon or musket discharge would cause her heart to stop. But she continued. At last, the farm came into view. The fighting in the area was fierce, and as she walked toward the building, a woman shouted, "Don't stand out in the line of fire, child. Get in here!"

Ella didn't need a second invitation. She scurried inside and found a group of women making bandages from sheets, baking bread, boiling large buckets of water, and laying out simple food to hand to soldiers. She sat down in a corner, and her head began to droop when a voice reproached her and said, "No time to rest. Make yerself useful."

"Yes, sorry," Ella said softly, and even though the weariness had seeped into her bones, she rose and worked at whatever task was required of her. The Union army had commandeered the farm now filled with the wounded and the dying. She blanched at the sight of so much blood, but quickly began to address the wounded men's needs, learning how to press down on a wound to stop the bleeding, clean the wounds and bind broken limbs.

She went about her work diligently for the rest of the day and night and into the next day, sleeping for a minute here and there. When the stench of blood, feces, infection, and general decay became overwhelming, she would quietly duck outside to vomit and return quickly, once more in the thick of things.

At one point, she found herself at the amputation table, something so alarming to the senses that one of the surgeon's aids made to shoo her away. "Get away with ye. This ain't no place for a wee lass, particularly one of your small frame."

Ella looked at him and refused to drop her gaze. She did not say a word, but neither did she leave. Finally, the man looked away. The need for aid was far greater than anyone had anticipated. No one else tried to make her go.

The next afternoon, she was at the well filling a cup with water for a wounded soldier lying in the shade of a tree when she heard someone shout, "Get that little bit of thing back in here. This one's not going to make it." Ella realized she was frequently called to the side of the dying. She would sit quietly with them, administering laudanum and sometimes singing softly as she stroked their feverish faces and held their hands. It was not the work that Ella wanted to be chosen for, but chosen she was, and she would serve where needed.

On the fourth day of the war, the absence of artillery and musket fire was both peaceful and eerie. Although many residents had attempted to bury the corpses during the night, bodies still covered the fields. The dead had been buried hastily, and foxes and coyotes made quick work at uncovering some of the remains. Ella was glad the battle seemed to be over, but then realized the actual work had just begun. As the victorious Union army marched south on the heels of the withdrawing Confederates, it took along most of the doctors, nurses, and able-bodied men who had worked alongside of the residents during the past days. Now the townspeople were left to deal with the overwhelming task ahead.

Ella could have gone with the army, but she had seen enough of war. Besides, she wanted to find Anna. Surely, she wouldn't have marched away without finding Ella to say farewell. Which meant, she knew, that Anna was either seriously wounded or dead. But she never found her.

The following weeks went by quickly. Besides tending to the wounded by bathing them, dressing their injuries, and feeding them, the women would grab shovels to help bury the ones who did not survive. Soldiers were treated and sent on their way when healed. Those needing more care were put on trains to Philadelphia, New York, and Baltimore.

By the end of August, the remaining three thousand wounded soldiers were moved to a large field hospital located in the northern corridor. Ella simply followed them and spent another three months tending to the decreasing numbers until finally, in the third week of November, it all was over. Ella knew she was no longer needed.

She stayed for a time with a family and worked as a healer, but Ella missed her home. So, on one cold, late-December day, she packed her kit and set out for Toronto, taking any mercy she found on the way. Eventually, after wandering along the Erie Canal, she located a steamer destined for Lake Ontario. She signed on as a cabin maid and worked for a pittance. Finally, when the town of Toronto came into view, perched on the northern side of giant Lake Ontario, Ella sank onto her knees and offered up a prayer of thanks.

She found that much had changed in her absence. Her family had lost their fortune, and now, with no dowry or desire to marry, she took work at the new hospital northwest of the city. She was proud of the experience she had gained as a civil war nurse. Later, Ella would enroll in the nursing school located on the grounds of the hospital. Since the war in America, nursing schools had begun to appear throughout both countries. This would be Ella's life-long career.

In the spring, she ventured to Anna's house to see if there was news. And news there was. Jacob had greeted her and told her Anna was very much alive and married to a farmer named Oswald. They lived just northwest of the city, not very far from the same hospital where Ella now served as a nurse.

"But she lost her arm," Jacob said sadly, "although she claims she can learn to shoot one-handed." He laughed. "You know Anna."

"She married Oswald? What did her stepmother think of that?"

"To quote the nasty woman, 'Why, Anna. Even *you* could have done better.' I thought Anna would knock the sneer right off her face, but she showed great restraint." They both laughed.

Then Jacob told her how he had barely escaped being kidnapped and had spent months looking for the two girls before sadly giving up. "But I will take you to her," he added excitedly. "It's not that far away."

July 2, 1867

Anna's brother, Jacob, sits on the front porch of the farmhouse playing with his beloved two-year-old niece, Annella, named in honor of the two friends. Anna and Ella are on the porch swing, sipping sherry and holding their faces to the setting sun. They are tired from all the festivities celebrating the union of Canada East and West along with the Maritime provinces into the new nation of Canada the previous day. It is a time of great excitement, but for the two young women, also a time of shared sorrow.

Since their return, they have met each July 2 to honor all those lost in America's great civil war. They sit silently for a time, each absorbed in her own thoughts.

"If we had not gone to fight, do you think our lives would be different now?" Anna asks.

"Yes, of course. I would be working as a servant somewhere, and you would be married to the *odious* man." They both laugh, but then sober.

The sun is setting beneath dark clouds and turning the sky various shades of deep pink, blue and grey, the promise of rain in the air. They hold their glasses of sherry aloft and toast Oswald's brother, Owen, who died that day on a hilltop in a small town called Gettysburg. They raise their glasses again to all men who died in the war that had blessedly ended in 1865. They toast a third time for the women who served and died as well.

And then, holding each other tight, they weep.

Author's note: An estimated forty thousand Canadians fought in the Civil War. They were of French and Anglo descent and some were of African descent. Four hundred of these were women from various parts of British North America (now Canada) dressed as soldiers to join the fray. The Canadians served in the infantry and on ships as enlistees, officers, doctors, and spies.

The reasons for joining were varied. The majority fought for the Union, but a minority sided with the southern cause. Money played a factor as the pre-war economy in British North America was poor and joining up was an opportunity for immediate cash and a pension later. Enterprising individuals north of the border also served in place of American citizens who were drafted but did not wish to fight. They paid their northern neighbors a good amount to act in their stead. And yes, crimpers did exist. They would cross the border, kidnap, and smuggle young men to the United States, where they sold them to nefarious recruiters.

An estimated seven thousand Canadians died in the Civil War. A monument to their bravery and sacrifice was erected in Cornwall, Ontario, in 2017 by the Grays and Blues of Montreal, a group known for preserving and understanding the role of the common soldier during the US Civil War.

Judith Cameron Seniura began her journalism career in the early '70s and has written for newspapers, magazines, and other media in Ontario, Canada, Alaska, Michigan, Nebraska, San Antonio, Marland, and Pennsylvania. This is her first published piece of fiction, but hopefully not her last.

Hidden Revenge

BY MARK GREATHOUSE

PROLOGUE - While the War Between the States raged, President Abraham Lincoln was necessarily distracted by the often-violent stirrings of savage tribes intent on fending off the seemingly endless migration of settlers and prospectors onto ancestral lands promised to them by the Great Father in Washington, D.C. No matter that the lands weren't the Great Father's to give. The Bureau of Indian Affairs hoped to broker peace by bringing a delegation of tribal chiefs to Washington to meet with the president. Meetings tended to be brief owing mostly to language barriers, so much of the chiefs' time was occupied with tours arranged by the government. As a matter of historical fact, the delegation headed back to their homes on April 30, 1863, but here is where our fiction begins. In this story, the delegation is rescheduled to head home on July 5, giving the chiefs the opportunity to visit a little town named Gettysburg behind the U.S. Army lines on July 3, 1863. The chiefs were tired from being on display and understandably frustrated at what they perceived as the duplicity and disinterest of the Great Father. Revenge by humanity's badly behaving children was in the air.

***

Chief Lean Bear of the Southern Cheyenne stared stoically at the onlookers who'd paid for the privilege of viewing genuine American savages at P. T. Barnum's American Museum in New York City. It was hard to judge what might be running through his mind. His thoughts most likely were to endure being Barnum's sideshow until he could return to the vast prairies, forests, and hills that were his heritage. He must have wondered what his wife and children might think were they to see him displayed like a circus sideshow. He was nevertheless decked out in his full ceremonial regalia from ornately beaded moccasins to a majestic feathered headdress. Several scalps hanging from Lean Bear's shield and lance added a sense of the savage macabre that Barnum fully exploited in attracting the crowds. Lean Bear's fellow chiefs represented bands of Comanche, Kiowa, Arapahoe, Caddo, and Cheyenne. The chiefs didn't need to speak, as their painted faces, buckskin scalp shirts, buffalo robes, long braids, ornate feathered headdresses, fringed leggings, and beaded moccasins spoke plenty loud enough for gawking crowds. They were at once diplomatic friends and sworn enemies of each other. The irony was palpable in the deferential ways they interacted. The paying customers were clueless as to the dynamic at work within the delegation. Barnum sensed it, but strove to keep the chiefs preoccupied while trumpeting the curious to come and see the chiefs before they returned forever to their wild frontier homes.

The four-tiered theater of Barnum's gallery on Broadway Street was regularly packed with a public both captivated and simply curious. Barnum, ever the showman, paraded his fierce-looking guests through the streets of Manhattan periodically along with a marching band to promote his guests.

They even stopped at local schools where children would perform for the delegation much to the delight of everyone. After having endured Barnum's patronizing but lucrative show, the chiefs expected to board a train for Denver on April 30. They surely craved the freedom of the wide-open spaces of their wilderness homes.

Chief Lean Bear was a leader of what was referred to among his people as the Council of Forty-Four. His Cheyenne name was *Awoninahku.* Although their decisions were non-binding, the Council of Forty-Four was a governing body viewed by the tribe as peacemakers. The label peacemaker might be subject to interpretation, as the Cheyenne trucked no aggressive incursions by neighboring tribes. The Cheyenne did have an aggressive part of the tribe called Dog Soldiers, and they accounted for much of the violence attributed even to the peaceful Cheyenne.

Chief Lean Bear and a handful of Council chiefs had received a visit nearly a year earlier from a contingent of soldiers. The term "unexpected visit" is used loosely, as few humans could approach an Indian encampment without being spotted. Lean Bear was thusly well prepared to meet these visitors. He stood impressively in full regalia, though wore no warpaint. He waited until the interlopers were within roughly 50 feet before raising his hand to call them to a halt. "You no blue coat." Lean Bear spoke broken English and simply expressed the Cheyenne's initial observation. These soldiers wore gray tunics. There were only a half dozen soldiers plus the driver of the accompanying wagon with its mule team. They appeared to be a bedraggled lot likely as a consequence of travel over rough terrain.

"Y'all are right, Chief. We fight your blue coat enemies."

Lean Bear was well aware that there was a war underway

far to the east and south. There were some Cheyenne chiefs who had seen this as an opportunity to halt the migration of white settlers into their ancestral lands, but the peacekeepers had advised against going on the warpath and, but for the Dog Soldiers, had mostly prevailed. Lean Bear saw no distinction between the gray coats and blue coats other than their uniform colors. They were soldiers. They were enemies to be wary of. The Cheyenne were vaguely aware of slavery being an issue, but it concerned them not as they practiced it themselves with prisoners from other tribes. He also surmised that once the war was over, the winning army would turn its attention back to persecuting his people.

"What do gray coats seek from Cheyenne?"

The Rebel lieutenant was surprised at Lean Bear getting right down to business. He'd expected some level of ceremony. The Indian agent had assured them that the Cheyenne were mostly peaceful.

"We give you guns to kill blue coats." The lieutenant conjured up an almost devious smile. "Have firewater, too."

The chief fought to keep from rolling his eyes at the soldier's sheer audacity. A quick glance at his fellow chiefs confirmed the response he'd already settled upon. "Gray coats go. Leave wagon here."

The lieutenant was quite aware of the contents of the wagon. Rifles, ammunition, whiskey, and other trade goods were to be traded in exchange for the Cheyenne becoming allies against the Yankees. "We cannot do that, Chief."

More than three dozen armed warriors appeared as if from thin air. War paint only served to enhance the threat imposed by nocked arrows and lances decorated with enemy scalps. Lean Bear gave as savage a glare as he could muster, so as to make sure his threat was clearly understood. "Go!

Now!" He deferentially swept his arm toward the trail from whence the gray coats had come.

The lieutenant reflexively ran his hand under his kepi as though assuring himself that he still had his hair. He glanced meekly at his fellow Rebels, shrugged ever so slightly, and led them away amidst an uneasy quiet.

Barely a year later on March 26, 1863, Indian agent Sam Colley and an interpreter accompanied Chief Lean Bear and the other tribal chiefs into the East Room of the White House. They had to negotiate a smoke-filled corridor filled with gawking diplomats, cabinet secretaries, journalists, and other invited guests. The delegation members seated themselves in a semi-circle on the carpet. The chiefs wore their best tribal trappings awash in intricate beadwork, soft yellow buckskin, luxurious fur, and colorful feathers. Only their lances, war clubs, and bows and arrows were missing and kept them from appearing overtly savage.

President Abraham Lincoln arrived 15 minutes late. He'd been reviewing reports of troop movements, an exercise that invariably left him frustrated. Having to face a collection of hostile Indians from the westernmost reaches of the nation was not exactly a desirable task at this moment. He'd been cursorily briefed enough to know that Lean Bear was the delegation leader.

Lincoln stood tall before the seated Indians. Colley was standing behind the chiefs and pointed at Lean Bear for the president's convenience. Lincoln reached out to offer his hand to the chief. "Pleasure to meet you." They shook hands tentatively, then purposefully. Lincoln wasted no time. "What do you have to say, Chief Lean Bear?"

The chief was momentarily taken aback, but gathered himself quickly and stood up. "Need chair."

Two chairs were brought in, and the chief and the president were duly seated opposite each other. There was an uncomfortable silence.

Lean Bear cradled a long-stemmed pipe which he finally lifted and swept the room as if holding some sort of pointer. He spoke in his halting but intelligible English. "We travel long way to hear counsel of Great Father. Cheyenne no fight blue coat, no fight gray coat. Live in peace. We live as one people." His eyes riveted in on Lincoln's, addressing him as an equal. He swept the room with his pipe once more. "Great Father chief of his people; live in big lodge. Lean Bear also great chief of his people."

Lincoln nodded his understanding, though was anxious for the chief to get to his point so he could get on with other presidential duties.

Lean Bear sensed Lincoln's impatience, but he was an orator among his people and wasn't about to shorten his remarks. He finally began to reach a conclusion to his speech. "Great Father must tell his white children to stop their attacks against my people, so both peoples can travel safely across our lands." The chief wasn't convinced that Lincoln was fully grasping his message. "Cheyenne... Kiowa... Comanche... Arapahoe... Caddo join in wishing for end to white men's great war." The reference to the ongoing insurrection seemed to resonate with Lincoln's sensibilities. "We must return to our homes, and we ask for the Great Father to offer peace and speed our travels."

The president smiled an awkward smile that bordered on condescension. "You have all spoken of the strange sights you see here, among your pale-faced brethren; the very great number of people that you see; the big wigwams; the difference between our people and your own. But you have seen but a very small part of the pale-faced people. You may wonder when I tell you that there are people here in this wigwam, now looking at you, who have come from other countries a great deal farther off than you have come. We pale-faced people think that this world is a great, round ball, and we have people here of the pale-faced family who have come almost from the other side of it to represent their nations here and conduct their friendly intercourse with us, as you now come from your part of the round ball." He'd had a globe brought into the room along with a professor who pointed out in basic terms the essence of land masses and seas.

Lincoln pointed to Europe and swept his hand across the globe to America. "Pale-faced people have journeyed far." His hand paused over the Great Plains. "You ask for my advice." Lincoln folded his hands and leaned toward Lean Bear. "We have people now present from all parts of the globe – here, and here, and here." Lincoln's fingers danced across the globe. "There is a great difference between this pale-faced people and their red brethren, both as to numbers and the way in which they live. We know not whether your own situation is best for your race, but this is what has made the difference in our way of living. The pale-faced people are numerous and prosperous because they cultivate the earth, produce bread, and depend upon the products of the earth rather than wild game for a subsistence. This is the chief reason of the difference; but there is another. Although we are now engaged in a great war between one another, we are not, as a race, so much disposed to fight and kill one another as our red brethren. You have asked for my advice. I really am not capable of advising you whether, in the providence of the Great Spirit, who is the great Father of us all, it is best for you to maintain the habits and customs of your race, or adopt a new mode of life. I can only say that I can see no way in which your race is to become as numerous and prosperous as the white race except by living as they do, by the cultivation of the earth. It is the object of this government to be on terms of peace with you, and with all our red brethren. We constantly endeavor to be so. We make treaties with you, and will try to observe them; and if our children should sometimes behave badly, and violate these treaties, it is against our wish. You know it is not always possible for any father to have his children do precisely as he wishes them to do. In regards to being sent back to your own country, we have an officer, the Commissioner of Indian Affairs, who will take charge of that matter, and make the necessary arrangements."[1]

***

The interpreter had been working hard to translate in a sign language he hoped most of the chiefs could grasp and was relieved to observe nods of understanding from the delegation.

Lincoln stood and extended his hand to Lean Bear and dutifully shook the hands of each of the other chiefs comprising the delegation. Each chief stood in turn to accept Lincoln's outreach. Bronzed-copper peace medals were handed out and papers attesting to the friendship between the government and the tribes were signed. The other Cheyenne chiefs, War Bonnet and Stands in the Water, glanced at Lean Bear as they shook the president's hand. The Kiowa had the largest delegation, including Yellow Buffalo, Lone Wolf, Yellow Wolf, White Bull, and Little Heart. The handshaking concluded with the Arapahoe chiefs Spotted Wolf and Nevah, Comanche chiefs Ten Bears and Pricked Forehead, the lone Apache chief Poor Bear and Caddo chief Jacob. As each chief's name was announced, it appeared that Lincoln's curiosity had been aroused such that he might have wondered how each had received their seemingly unusual names. The president nevertheless impressed the chiefs with the firmness of his handshake, a sign that exuded trust. Notably, the Kiowa squaws Etta and Coy were not introduced, as that would have been inappropriate per Indian custom given their view as to the role of women in their culture. The treatment of women by both races was in many ways not all that different.

The delegation spent the next two weeks being shuttled around the various impressive government buildings and forts around Washington before heading off to fulfill their promise to P. T. Barnum in New York. The train ride from Washington was like a prequel to Barnum's show in the big city, as crowds gathered at each station where the train was obliged to slow down or even stop.

Regrettably, the Kiowa chief Yellow Wolf caught pneumonia and passed away on April 7, casting a distinct pall over the adventure to the east. The remaining Kiowas were of a mind to leave early, but Barnum coaxed them to stay. They were nearing the planned departure date and the showman sought to milk the Indians for every possible advantage.

Chief Lean Bear called a meeting of the delegation. They arranged to meet on a grassy knoll north of New York City well out of earshot of Barnum and the government representatives.

Ever the showman, Barnum suggested that they were plotting to go on the warpath in New York City, but his joke was quickly rebuffed.

Lean Bear drew the chiefs close. "The pale face Barnum has invited us to stay longer. Two moons. He show us Boston and Philadelphia and place called Baltimore. He says he will give us great gifts to take back to our people."

The Kiowa chief Lone Wolf spoke up, "Our people worry

about us. We must return soon."

Lean Bear's smile revealed a man comfortable with himself and brimming with the confidence that comes with long experience in these matters. His way was always to promote peaceful settlement of issues. He figured the loss of the remaining four Kiowas would reduce the size of the delegation slightly but not diminish Barnum's overall plans. Besides, he had begun to crave the white man's gifts. "If brave Kiowa wish to leave... go." He wasn't able to prevent his facial expression from revealing his disappointment.

When the other chiefs revealed their desire to stay, the Kiowas reluctantly changed their minds.

Over the next two months, Barnum paraded the delegation in the major northeastern cities. As the commitment drew to a close, and the delegation anxiously looked forward to a departure of July 5, the Commissioner of Indian Affairs stepped in for one last convincing display of the white man's military might. William Dole, a strong proponent of forging treaties with the Indians and moving them to reservations, heard of some sort of major incursion by the Confederate Army at a little farm town in south-central Pennsylvania. He enthusiastically seized the opportunity and shepherded the delegation by train to Baltimore and then in a caravan of four large carriages to the Gettysburg. They arrived at the break of dawn on July 3.

Dole strode across the grassy knoll with the Indian delegation behind him in full regalia. He was understandably uneasy. As Commissioner for Indian Affairs, it was his duty to assuage the frustrations of the thirteen tribal chiefs and two squaws he'd lured to Washington with promises of peace for their people. He knew a costly war raged. There was hardly a place untouched by its writhing tentacles that seemed to suck the life from anything the insurrection touched. The Plains Indians were no exception. Dole heard that the major Rebel force that had arrived at Gettysburg was positioning for a decisive battle aimed at carrying the Rebel cause directly to the northeastern states. Chalk it up to a certain naivete, but it was clear that he had no appreciation for the degree of distraction that his delegation of savages brought to an already tense situation.

General George Meade's eyes riveted like steel spikes into those of the commissioner. His face reddened. "What the hell could you have been thinking, Dole?" He knew the chiefs could hear every word, but he didn't give a tinker's damn whether they understood English.

The commissioner was torn between standing tall as a show of strength for the delegation versus cowering under Meade's anger.

The general wasn't about to be distracted a moment longer. "See those trees over there on the knoll? That's Culp's Hill. Keep your damned savages out of sight behind those trees."

The general abruptly made an about face, muttered something under his breath, and stalked off to attend to battle preparations. The Rebels had quite clearly been gathering forces all morning for some sort of assault and demanded his full attention.

Dole dutifully directed the delegation toward the trees on Culp's Hill. It afforded a vantage point from which the chiefs could barely view the battle that was to come. The delegation dutifully squatted in a line just in front of a gnarled old tree with its spreading limbs affording a modicum of shade.

General Meade reluctantly assigned a couple of soldiers to stand guard, both to ensure that no harm came to the government guests and, of greater concern, that they stay put. He didn't need a bunch of heathen Indians mucking up his defenses in the heat of battle.

The chiefs sat patiently. Dole had already begun to regret that he'd extended the delegation's stay and come to this now godforsaken place. Culp's Hill was not an ideal vantage point to view the impending battle. Finally, in the early afternoon, the roar of Confederate cannon tore the pre-battle quietude apart. The Rebel yells soon followed, as waves of butternut and gray swept toward Cemetery Ridge and into a devastating defensive barrage. Grape... cannister... and musket fire riddled the Rebel ranks. Yet they charged on.

It was as though the very earth was exploding as the din of battle reached the ears of the chiefs. Their eyes were transfixed by what little they could see of the battle, as some stood stretching tall to take it in and communicating excitedly with hand signs in reaction to the conflagration unfolding before them. Given the considerably smaller scope of most Plains Indian battles, the sheer magnitude of the clash of humanity before them was overwhelming to their senses. It was not long, and much to the nervous concern of the two soldiers guarding them, before the entire delegation was standing so as to better view the scene. More troubling, they began to inch toward the battle.

Chief Lean Bear realized that he needed to relieve himself. He nudged War Bonnet standing beside him and pointed to his own breechcloth. With everyone focused on the melee before them, he broke from the delegation, eased over behind the gnarled old tree, pulled his breechcloth aside, and peed on a tree root.

"What the hell you doin' over here, ya damn savage?" One of the assigned guards had noticed the chief's departure and chased after him. The soldier was a corporal and an older one at that. He spat a load of chewing tobacco juice from under his broad mustache. "Get yer sorry ass back with them other heathens!" he snarled as he pulled back the hammer on his musket. He'd done a bit of fighting out west and learned early on of the increasingly accepted advice that the only good Indian was a dead Indian. He had no concern with the niceties of diplomacy and fully no respect for any status afforded a Cheyenne chief. An Indian was an Indian.

Lean Bear had grown tired of this odyssey into the white man's great kingdom. His patience had grown paper thin. The pale faces' big cities and curious crowds had long ago lost his interest. The conflagration playing out on the fields of Gettysburg proved to him that the white man was no better than the red man. His eyes riveted in on the corporal. "Me no finish."

"Damn! An Injun what speaks like a white man!" The soldier offered up a derisive laugh but had the misfortune of losing his grip on the musket. It was an old firearm likely handed down within his family. The barrel was just a tad slick from the humidity. As he caught it, the stock hit the ground, the hammer released, struck the frizzen, and the musket accidently discharged its payload into the sky. The sound of the shot was lost in the din of the battle.

Lean Bear reacted instinctively to what he perceived as an attack. His knife blade appeared in his hand and slashed savagely across the corporal's belly.

The soldier looked down at his stomach, his face contorted with pain. "Damn! I be bleedin'!" It was a serious cut but not a mortal wound. The severity mattered none to him. His musket was now no better than a club. "You damned Injun'!" He gripped the barrel and began to raise it over his head.

The chief moved catlike to within inches of the corporal.

He was too close for the soldier to club him, and his knife found the soldier's throat. A quick thrust and slice ended the fight. Lean Bear looked about. Apparently, no one had seen the brief altercation.

Lean Bear dragged the soldier's body behind the tree and out of direct line of sight. He figured it likely that the body wouldn't be discovered until after the battle. The chief took one last look around and was preparing to head back to the delegation when instinct overcame him. He stood over the fallen corporal and grasped the man's golden locks. A few deft slices of the knife, and Chief Lean Bear had himself a blue coat scalp. He looked around cautiously once more and stuffed the scalp into his wampum bag. There was no point in drawing attention to a fresh scalp hanging from his waistband. He took a final look at the dead soldier, placed the corporal's kepi back on his head, gave a smile of triumph, turned, and walked confidently back to the delegation.

He sidled up to War Bonnet and caught the fellow Cheyenne's eye. Lean Bear permitted himself a satisfied smile, as he glanced down at his wampum bag. A small blotch of fresh blood stained the lower portion of the bag.

War Bonnet's eyes quickly noted the tell-tale evidence of the chief's encounter. He couldn't contain a smile, as he sensed the same justice as Lean Bear.

The huge battle before the assembled chiefs raged on, the gray line at one point nearly breaking through the blue coat defenses and causing some concern to the Indians. Through it all, the delegation stood as stoically as they could muster.

A lieutenant walked by, his bloodied arm hanging loosely by his side. He looked at the remaining soldier guarding the delegation. "Where the hell is Smith, soldier?" His eyes scanned the delegation. "He run off again?"

Lean Bear could barely contain a triumphant smile.

The lieutenant didn't wait for an answer. "We'll find him later. Watch yourself." He stared hard at Commissioner Dole. "Damn politicians!" He strode off.

The battle finally came to an end with the Rebels in full retreat. Like the Indians so often were guilty of, General Meade didn't follow up on his advantage by pursuing and destroying the enemy. Dole was relieved to have survived unscathed and hoped to leave the scene unnoticed. The carriages were already being brought toward Culp's Hill.

General Meade caught sight of the carriages and instantly figured them as potential ambulances. "You there... Colonel!" He called out to Colonel Colvill, who'd most recently repelled the Rebel advance at The Angle on Cemetery Ridge. "Commandeer those damned carriages!"

The colonel was bone tired but wasn't about to challenge a direct order from the commanding general. He turned his horse toward Culp's Hill and was soon waving to get the attention of the approaching carriages. As the colonel rode in front of the Indian delegation, Commissioner Dole finally showed some spine. He waved a piece of paper at Colvill.

"You can't have them, Colonel!" He was nearly bowled over by the colonel's horse. "Got direct orders from President Lincoln!"

The recent heat of battle coupled with Dole's resistance was too much for Colvill. The Indian chiefs in all their finery threatened to put his mental state over the top. "I've got wounded men to tend to. Who the hell are you?" He looked over his shoulder and saw General Meade watching him. "Damn it, man. Give me at least two of those contraptions."

Dole rightly figured discretion was the better part of valor. His charges could be squeezed into two carriages for the ride back to Baltimore. "I'm Commissioner of Indian Affairs for the United States Government, Colonel. It would be my pleasure to part with two of my carriages to assist in recovering our valiant wounded soldiers." Dole swiftly directed the two lead carriages away from the delegation, while the chiefs piled into the remaining carriages. He had the abbreviated caravan headed out before General Meade could react.

Colvill caught Meade's resigned expression and led his newly acquired ambulances toward Cemetery Ridge. As he turned his horse away from Culp's Hill, the colonel's peripheral vision caught a pair of legs sticking out behind the largest of the stand of trees on the hill. He brought his mount around and cantered over to the tree. As he peered down, he couldn't miss the dead Union soldier lying behind it. He dismounted. Blood had streamed down the sides of the corporal's head. Suspicious, the colonel respectfully lifted the dead man's kepi. He stepped back aghast. The soldier's scalp was missing!

The Indian delegation had already lumbered from sight.

Colvill sprang into the saddle with renewed energy and rode hard toward General Meade. "General! General, sir! A word!" he hollered.

"At ease, Colonel. What the hell has you so all-fired upset? There's plenty enough of that to go round at this hour." Meade's horse nearly dumped him from the saddle, as it took an unexpected sidestep to avoid a dead soldier. The general brought his mount back under control. "Out with it, Colonel."

The colonel caught his breath. "Scalped, sir! One of those heathen savages... they scalped one of our men!"

Anger flashed across Meade's face. Sweat was streaming down his cheeks, and his uniform was soaked. He scanned the field with its hundreds of bloody corpses and tried to block his ears from the moans and desperate screams of the wounded. The horrific odor of battle, of death, still lingered in the air. As though post-battle clean-up wasn't enough, a new challenge had now found its way into his consciousness. He sighed heavily, muttering a few curses under his breath. "Write it up, Colonel... Colvill, is it? Make sure no one here sees that our man was scalped." Politics and its intrigues were not unknown to Meade. He'd have to take this up personally with President Lincoln.

Lean Bear nudged War Bonnet, as their carriage lumbered its way toward Baltimore and the train that would soon be carrying them westward to their homelands. He turned back the flap on his wampum bag enough for his friend to peer inside at the ball of hair and flesh nestled inside.

War Bonnet nodded approvingly and offered up an uncharacteristic smile. He asked in the Cheyenne tongue, "Did you count coup?" War Bonnet was concerned that Lean Bear had exhibited bravery by touching the blue coat, counting coup before killing him.

The chief winked and made a slashing motion with his hand. "Yes. Make good story at council." The chief was adept at wrapping engaging stories around his combat prowess, and his surreptitious and fully unexpected engagement at Gettysburg would serve him well before the council fire flames. Another feather would soon be added to the plumage of his already impressive headdress.

By now, their companions in the carriage had started to become aware of Lean Bear's accomplishment. Murmurs of approval found their way from chief to chief.

Soon enough, the stirrings reached Commissioner Dole. He reflexively turned toward Lean Bear with an inquisitive look.

The chief opened his wampum bag and extended it toward Dole.

The smell and blood stain at the bottom of the bag were enough to repel the commissioner. "What the hell have you done!?" It was rhetorical. The chief's accomplishment was quite obvious. Dole shook his head dismayingly. He saw resignation from office in his future.

A broad smile creased Lean Bear's face as though challenging the commissioner to do anything about it. The chiefs were tired. Tired of the politicians, tired of the shows filled with curiosity seekers, tired of the pale faces showing off their military might, tired of seemingly endless days away from their people. The chief grew serious and shrugged. He finally strove to make light of the situation as he pointed to the commissioner's long dark hair, made a slicing motion, and held out the wampum bag. A murmur of approval emanated from the delegation followed by light laughter that broke the tension.

A chill found its way up Dole's spine. He looked questioningly at the chief as though trying to ascertain whether he might be serious.

Lean Bear caught the commissioner's eyes, smiled innocently, and mustered a bit of a twinkle. "We have problem?" he asked.

"Just hide that damned thing when we get on the train." He resignedly shook his head.

July 5 arrived in the nick of time, so far as the delegation and Indian Affairs Commission were concerned. Between Colonel Colvill not getting to his report until late in the evening and General Meade's concerns with other matters, the incident on Culp's Hill arrived at the White House far too late to do anything about it.

It had been a long day for Abraham Lincoln. He broke the seal of the leather pouch and drew out a sheaf of papers that included Meade's report of the third day at Gettysburg. Despite being dead tired, the president dutifully skimmed through the report by candlelight. It pleased him that General Lee's forces had been repelled and sent into a full-blown retreat. He shook his head with frustration upon reading of Meade's plans to spend a couple of days regrouping his troops before pursuing General Lee's retreating Confederate Army. He mumbled under his breath about being unable to find a field general that was capable of pursuing and finishing off a retreating enemy. Lincoln nearly didn't notice a piece of paper that yet remained in the pouch. Given what he'd just read, the report from a Colonel Colvill actually brought a wry smile to his lips. He thought on his words to Chief Lean Bear about children behaving badly and it not always being possible for any father to have his children do precisely as he wishes them to do. It seemed the Indian delegation had indeed behaved badly. Still bemused by the irony, he shook his head. There was little to be done about it now.

Lean Bear's arrival in Denver was cause for considerable celebration, as more than a hundred Cheyenne had made the long trek from their most recent encampment in central Kansas. The other members of the delegation received similar greetings from their respective tribes as they raised the medallions Lincoln had gifted them with.

Lean Bear was relieved to finally be mounted on his favorite pony. He led his assembled people aside, so he could enjoy the reunion with his people out of sight of the Indian Affairs agents that had accompanied them on the train. His fellow Cheyenne chiefs Stands in the Water and War Bonnet rode on either side as Lean Bear triumphantly hoisted his prized scalp with its attached long blond hair. A great roar of approval went up as though ignorant of the peace-keeping nature of their journey. They would be encamped many miles from Denver, when the chief finally had the opportunity to recount the tale of his encounter with the blue-coat corporal.

After the sun had sunk below the horizon in a gaudy blaze of orange, Lean Bear stood before the great council fire and pantomimed his sneaking away from the delegation on Culp's Hill. He described his stalking the blue-coat corporal, conveniently leaving out his purpose as having been to answer nature's call. He told of the blue-coat's shooting his musket and missing the chief thanks to his superior medicine. The chief paused theatrically before showing how he counted coup before slitting the soldier's throat and taking his scalp. He smiled deviously upon telling how the white soldiers were unaware of his mighty deed. The Cheyenne hooted and howled approval of Lean Bear's accomplishment. Naturally, the story would be embellished, as he told it every night until they reached the main village in central Kansas.

***

EPILOGUE - On May 16, 1864, a bit less than 15 months after having met President Lincoln in Washington, Lean Bear, Black Kettle, War Bonnet, and others in the tribe were encamped near Ash Creek in central Kansas. The 1st Colorado Regiment under the command of Lieutenant George Eayre, approached the encampment with its 400 warriors. Despite a bloody fight having occurred a few weeks back involving aggressive Cheyenne Dog Soldiers at Fremont's Orchard, Chief Lean Bear was confident that the violence would not be linked to his peaceful tribe. He was certain that this would be a peaceful encounter, so he rode out alone to meet the soldiers and show his peaceful intentions. On his chest, the chief even displayed his peace medal that he had received on his trip to Washington D.C. In his hand, he held an official document signed by President Lincoln stating that he was peaceful and friendly with whites. Unbeknownst to Lean Bear, Eayre's troops were operating under orders from Colonel John Chivington to "kill Cheyennes whenever and wherever found." Chivington had necessarily knuckled to complaints by Colorado Governor John Evans. The 1st Colorado Regiment responded over-enthusiastically to Chivington's orders, as they arrayed eighty-six men and two-howitzers before Lean Bear's encampment. Eayre summarily ordered his men to shoot Lean Bear. The wounded chief fell from his horse and then was shot multiple times by the soldiers as they rode past his body. The troops went on to attack the surprised Cheyenne in the encampment. Before too much damage could be wreaked, Black Kettle emerged to de-escalate the situation, and the troops retreated to Fort Larned. Thus, it was that government ignorance and treachery intersected with Indian trust and naivete to prolong the conflict between the red man and white man across the American plains.

[1]Lincoln's words in this paragraph and the next are direct quotations from *Lincoln's Speech to the Indians*, from Basler, Roy P., *The Collected Works of Abraham Lincoln*. The Abraham Lincoln Association, Springfield, Illinois, vol. 6, New Brunswick, N.J.: Rutgers Univ. Press, 1953.

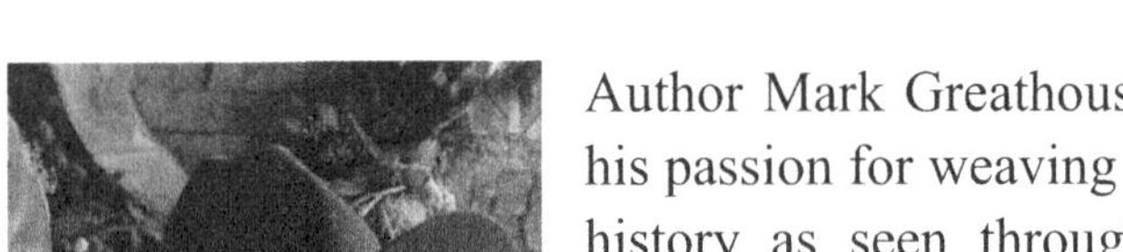

Author Mark Greathouse continues his passion for weaving fiction with history as seen through his short story *Hidden Revenge: Children Behaving Badly*. Whether expressed in his epic western genre Tumbleweed Saga novels or adventure-laced biographies, he couples a soul-penetrating creative spirit with extensive historical research. Greathouse is a member of Western Writers of America, the Gettysburg Writers Brigade, and several poetry societies. He delivers life-impacting YouTube videos at Tumbleweed.me and on Facebook at Tumbleweed Sagas and at Ask Tumbleweed. He holds degrees from University of Maryland (BA) and The American University (MBA). Learn of Greathouse's copy editing services for authors and publishers at Tumbleweed.me. The author lives in Southern Pennsylvania and dreams of retiring to the Texas Hill Country and further connecting with his Texas family roots.

Loved You Before: The Jack and Daisy Story

BY GREG SPICKA

A Forced Journey

It's a clear autumn dusk sky just outside of Little Easton in Essex, England, 1943, and Jack is happy to be wrapping up another flying mission over Europe in the B-26 marauder. He always enjoys looking at the red and orange horizon just before landing. Another nice landing makes him feel good and gives his crew more confidence in him. He lets the copilot taxi over to their parking spot and idle the engines down. The pilots go through the daily routine of turning all the switches and dials then turning the engines off. The crew sits in silence for a few minutes to gather their thoughts; they're back again.

The ground crews start opening the plane's doors while examining the exterior for any damage.

"Hey, no holes this time," says one of the ground crew.

"Did you at least hit your target?" snaps one guy.

Jack's navigator, Bill, jumps out of the front of the plane and looks at him. "We sure did! Blew that train right off the tracks."

The ground crew cheers. Bill slaps the side of the plane's nose. "You can put the train silhouette here, right next to these little factory ones, and this little boat, and a couple of these planes. Finally, a train on this girl."

A Jeep stops in front of the B-26 bomber and the driver looks at a paper. "Capt. Jack Flanders! The Colonel wants to see you in his office after the debriefing."

Jack gives a gentle nod of approval. "I'll be there."

"I wonder what that's all about," his copilot Jim says while putting his hands on his hips.

"We will find out later." Jack picks up his belongings and starts walking to the building.

After the debriefing, Jack heads over to the colonel's office. In the hallway, he sees Captain Ted Benton. "So, you're summoned also?"

Ted looks confused. "Wonder what's up? Probably us flying low again. We seem to scare some people. Negligent flying is what I've been told. We have had no problems since doing it."

Jack nods his head in agreement. "But it works. It gets us home every time."

The door to the colonel's office opens and a voice booms. "Gentlemen, come on in."

Jack and Ted take off their caps, tuck them under their left arm and then snap to attention, saluting the colonel.

"At ease." He throws a manila folder on his desk. "Gentlemen, we have orders to send you stateside."

Jack and Ted look at each other in confusion.

"Sir?" Jack turns to the colonel. "We have not finished our tour yet. I'm only twenty missions in so far."

"I know, but the two of you are the best that I have and there are a handful of other pilots from other squadrons that are being pulled, too. Looks like you're going to be training others in the heavies. The tree top level flying you have been pulling off? Well, word has gotten back stateside and they want you to train for something big next year."

Jack reaches down and picks up the folder with his name on it and glances over the orders. "Harrisburg, Pennsylvania? B-24s? Ted, we are going to fly the liberators."

"Whoa, those are heavies. But what do we know of flying them?" Ted questions. "I mean, sure I can learn to fly them no problem, but why us?"

"Surely there are more qualified pilots than Ted and I. Pilots who started in them could train new pilots?"

The colonel puts both hands on his desk, looks at them, and calmly says, "I know; I argued the same point. But what the two of you have is what the others don't. Experience. Experience flying over enemy territory with fighters and ground fire of all sorts shooting at you. And you make it back every time."

He walks over to them, puts his hand out to shake theirs, and congratulates them.

"You leave tomorrow. It has been nice serving with you, and I know you will make this unit proud."

Jack and Ted salute and head out of the building.

"Huh. Wonder how my crew will take my leaving them," Ted says.

Jack looks through the orders. "Well, it sounds like they are coming with us. They have navigation, bomb site, and gunner experience. After all, we just fly the plane. They do all the hard work."

"That is a relief. Guess we will break the news to them," Ted says.

Jack has an idea. "Why don't we get the crews together and tell them all at once? Might be easier on us."

"Agreed."

"And it looks like we are getting promoted to major. Imagine that."

Stateside Wonders

Brenda and Daisy are best friends and nurses at the Annie Warner hospital in Gettysburg. Their shift comes to an end, and they leave in Daisy's car to get a bite to eat.

"So Brenda. How's the farmer guy you are dating?"

"Oh, just fine. But the real question is when are you going to date?" Brenda turns herself sideways on the large car seat to face Daisy. Daisy quickly changes the subject back to her.

"Just fine? That doesn't sound like actual love."

"Eh, not really, but it's just something to pass the time. You know." Brenda taps Daisy's shoulder in a teasing way. "Why are you avoiding the question? You are almost thirty, right?"

Daisy doesn't answer. She knows thirty years is a long time to stay single. But how could she tell her best friend that she feels like she's waiting for someone—the someone? Brenda would think she's totally a lost cause. They pull into a filling station. A young attendant opens their car doors and starts filling the gas tank while the two ladies go inside. Their nursing uniforms caught the attention of two young men who came over and started bothering them with bad pickup lines.

***

Since Jack's family is back in the Midwest, he decides to stay at the Capitol City Airport in Harrisburg to watch the 7th fighter squadron and some of the photo reconnaissance aircraft train. The second day, a sergeant offers Jack his car to just go for a drive, saying it will be good for him to get into "normal" clothes for once.

Jack drives and soon finds himself outside of the town of Gettysburg, oddly being pulled to this place. So he figures he will check out the town and battlefields. Jack's not sure of the street he parked on, but walks to Cemetery Hill and all the monuments were amazing to him. He wonders how all those men and boys did it, fighting among themselves. His thoughts soon turned to the battlefield he had just left. Jack's battlefield is the skies over Europe, and he feels a little guilty being stateside now.

Jack continues to walk along the roadside out of town until he comes across a filling station. Wondering if they have a nice cold pop he has been craving for some time, he wanders in.

"Hey, you got any cold pop?"

The older man standing beside the counter holding a newspaper points over to the red and white Coke chest on the floor. Jack opens the lid, pulls out a cold bottle, and pops the cap on the side of the cooler. *There's that nice fizzing sound I've been waiting for.*

But before Jack can get the cool refreshment to his lips, a lady says, "No, now let us be!"

"Come on, miss, you can have a lot of fun with us." A young man blocks her from leaving the store.

Jack looks over to see two women, one with curly

blonde hair and the other a brunette, both about five feet tall or so, being held back by two younger men. He finishes taking the gulp of soda, sets it aside, and calmly walks over to them.

"Now I'm not going to be a hero or anything, but I suggest you let the lovely ladies go on their way." Jack had that firm look about him. He meant business.

"Well, look at here, Sticks," the young man says as he taps the other thin man's chest. "We got us an objector, or are you scared to join the army?"

Jack becomes furious at that notion, calling him a coward or an objector for those that refused to fight in the war, but his experience overcomes what he wanted to do to the young man.

"Damn right, I'm afraid," he says, convicted.

The two men give a small laugh, but before they can say anything, Jack continues with a louder voice.

"I was terrified every morning I got up before dawn and wondered who was I going to kill today on the ground during my bombing run. Was I going to get one of my men killed on this flight? Damn right, I'm afraid. Struggling to dodge all the flak. Gunfire from the ground. Other planes shooting at us while being stuck in a small aluminum box full of fuel and bombs. Moving at over 300 miles per hour. Working to keep the plane from crashing at every moment."

Jack lifts his shirt and reveals some burn marks and holes that are healing.

"And the hot metal slicing through your copilot and some of his body parts ending up in you. Take a good look, boys. I said inside you! Yea, that's right. I am afraid. But not afraid of ripping you two yucks apart, because I've seen worse."

***

The two young men, now silent, also see Jack's 45 side arm under his jacket and now know he is still active. They quickly apologize to the women and to Jack, then make their way to the door to leave. Jack slowly tucks his shirt back in and looks at the lady with the curly blonde hair staring at him.

"Did that really happen?" says the brunette.

"Every bit of it. I wish I was making it up."

Jack pauses for a second, looking into the blonde's yellowish green eyes. *Those are amazing eyes.* He had an odd sense that he couldn't explain. He grabs his pop, pays for it, and leaves, doing a double take at the blonde.

"Ooo Daisy, he has a thing for you."

"Umm, huh? No, he doesn't."

"Sure he does. The way he was looking back at you? And that swept back black hair, and that chiseled face. Oh, he is a dreamboat."

Daisy stands there watching Jack walk away, thinking he was cute and friendly. She has an odd feeling about the whole encounter but can't place anything yet.

"So you do like him." Brenda pokes her in the arm, and Daisy comes to from her daydreaming.

The next day, Jack has more free time and has this itching desire to go back to Gettysburg. It is about midday, and he walks around near the square and heads down Chambersburg Street. Growing hungry and parched, he stops at the Blue Parrot. The building is smaller than what he was used to back home, but Jack can smell the great food and beer, and his cravings come on real quick for some solid food.

He sits down at the bar, looking at the black-and-white checkered floor when a man comes over to him.

"Hey, I want to show you something," he states.

"What's that?"

"Well, I have been coming in here for a long time. I got to know a lot of good people." He points at some pictures on the wall, walks to one particular one, and taps it with his finger. "I also got to know the story behind some of these pictures, and this one, well, this has me beside myself."

"And why is that?" Jack asks.

"Hopefully you could answer that for me."

"Now, how could I do that? I had never been here before." Thinking, this is some kind of trick, he stays in his seat.

A waitress comes walking by and looks at the picture, then at Jack. "Wow, that is uncanny."

Curiosity gets the best of him, and he looks at the picture. To his astonishment, it is an old black-and-white photo taken from the Civil War era. A man and a woman stand side by side for a photograph. The man looks like Jack in a blue Union uniform. Jack stands there in amazement.

"I see. That does look like me. But the girl looks as if she has curly blonde hair, do you think?"

"Well, that's the other funny part—"

"She is so beautiful," Jack interrupts. "But she... she looks like the lady I saw at the filling station yesterday." He softly puts his finger over her on the picture, making sure it is real. "She had the most incredible yellowish green eyes. Like a field of flowers that you want to get lost in, and if that was me, I never would want to find my way out of. I mean, you would take care of someone like that, very special and beautiful."

"Ah um," says the man, tapping him on the shoulder. "That is the other part." He steps aside, and there, standing behind him, is the lady in the nurse's uniform.

"Oh… ah. I mean… Yes, you are beautiful. Oh my." Jack stumbles over his words while bringing his hand up to scratch the back of his head. "Well, it looks like you."

She is blushing and amused at the same time and gets close to Jack to see the picture. She smiles at him as she slowly passes him. But she stares at Jack instead of looking at the picture. When she speaks, her lovely voice goes straight to Jack's heart and has him instantly hooked.

"You were that guy yesterday at the filling station, right?"

"Yes, I was. Um... Are you going to glance at the picture?"

She turns to see. "That really looks like me. And you too. How can that be?"

"I don't know," says the man.

"Who are they?" asks Jack.

"We are not sure, but soon after this was taken, the battle of Gettysburg happened. He was killed and some say she died weeks later of a broken heart."

"That's awful and sad," Daisy says.

"Yes, it is, but who are you two?" the man asks curiously.

"I'm Jack." He pulls out his hand to shake the guy's hand.

She is staring at Jack. "I'm Daisy."

Jack instinctively reaches out to shake her hand, as he does with everybody. When their hands touch, they both feel a tingle in their arms and an energetic twitch in their soul as if they belong together somehow. She looks deep into his blue-gray eyes while he gazes at hers. Before long, both hands are holding each other as if it happened naturally.

"Well, this is something indeed," says the man as he turns to leave them alone.

"They make a cute couple alright," the waitress says, walking by with a plate of food.

A couple? Jack thinks. *She is something special alright.*

I could see myself holding on to him, Daisy thinks. *I just met the guy, but I seem so comfortable around him.*

Jack releases her hands and asks if she would join him. She responds she has company with her. Somewhat disappointed but still wanting to spend time with her, he asks, "Why don't you bring him over too?"

"Oh. no, no, no," Daisy says laughing. "She is my friend Brenda from yesterday."

Jack is relieved to hear that and the three of them sit at the bar together. She asks what he is doing here. He explains he is in Harrisburg for the next few months to train pilots and crew to fly the B-24s. Daisy explains she is a nurse in Gettysburg at the Annie Warner hospital and lives on her uncle's farm east of town. The two go on forever with stories of who they are, what they have done, and both are deep into each other's conversation.

Brenda, the older man, and the waitress are standing back and taking all this in.

"I have never seen Daisy like this. She is usually so quiet."

"It is like they're old friends catching up," the man stated.

After an hour, Brenda taps Daisy's shoulder and reminds her that they need to get to work. Not realizing how much time has gone by, Daisy hurriedly gets up and looks at Jack like she really doesn't want to leave.

"Perhaps I could see you tomorrow?" Jack says. "Meet you for lunch?"

A smiling Daisy replies, "Sure, that would be nice. Noon?"

On the drive back to the base, the only thing Jack can

think of is Daisy and her curly blonde hair. The scent of her when she was close leaves him with a huge grin, and he cannot wait for tomorrow's meeting. When he sees Ted, he tells him all about her and the strange picture. It surprises Ted to see Jack all excited like this.

All through work, Daisy and Brenda gossip about Jack, the picture, and how they met. She is so giddy to see him tomorrow.

That evening, Daisy and Jack both think about each other and what to do next. Jack feels emotions he has not had before. Daisy is usually hesitant about guys she meets, but with Jack she oddly knows to give him a go.

Not Soon Enough

The next day, they meet at the Blue Parrot again. After a short time, she takes him back to her uncle's farm and they stroll through the growing corn fields, the apple tree rows, and barns. Daisy shows him her favorite spot to rest at the arched walking bridge over the stream that is at least fifty feet wide and only ten feet tall. In the next few weeks, this bridge becomes their meeting spot, and they always take a walk through the fields when they have time to get together.

They soon discover they have a lot in common, and when both are away, they can't wait to meet at the farm again. Jack ends up spending time here whenever he is not on duty, sometimes just coming down and helping her uncle out while Daisy is at work. One evening before he leaves, Jack is quiet.

"Why are you so quiet?" The silence between them grows. "Jack?"

"Well, the next two weeks are going to be non-stop training for the men. I won't be able to come by and visit." He stares at the passing water under the bridge and watches a leaf float by, tumbling in the water.

They peer into each other's eyes, yearning for a kiss that doesn't come. Neither one wants to start the kiss, but both are desiring it.

"It's okay Jack. It's just training. You can come back after it's all over."

He hugs her and holds her tight for what seemed like an hour, with all kinds of thoughts going through his mind about what this is, how Daisy is perfect for him, and how he desires to be with her every moment of the waking day.

After weeks of training the men, Jack takes them on a low-flying practice run. They leave Harrisburg, get to bombing altitude, pretend to bomb Hanover, and then dive quickly and make a hard right to the west. Flying at treetop level, Jack leads them to Daisy's uncle's farm and turns right to go north and east, back to Harrisburg. The bombers flying over so low and fast amaze Daisy and her uncle.

Summer goes by, and it is early September. Three weeks have passed since Daisy and Jack saw each other. She is waiting on the bridge like she has been since they started going steady a few months back. Jack drives the car down the lane slowly. It was uncharacteristic of him to take his time to get out of the car. She knows something is wrong almost instantly. He strolls over to her with one hand in his pocket and the other behind his back.

Walking up to her, he pulls out a dozen roses for her. She smiles with joy and smells them.

"What are these for?"

"After all this time, I have been so infatuated with you—you are all I can think about—that I forgot about the basic dating stuff."

"Okay, thank you for the flowers. But what is wrong,

Jack?"

She pulls herself up to him as close as she can get and he knows she wants an answer. He takes a deep breath and smiles.

"They have handed me my transfer papers. We leave for England in three days."

She stands there in silence. A tear forms in her eye. She lets the roses fall to the bridge floor, and two roll off into the water below, slowly floating away. She puts her head on his chest while he holds her in his arms. They stand there until the sun sets and the moon rises in the midnight blue of the night, taking over the deep red-orange of the twilight.

She looks up at him and whispers, "After all this time, how come you haven't kissed me yet?"

He looks into her eyes and says, "I have been wanting to since the first time I saw you. I wanted to taste those luscious lips of yours while squeezing you tight, but I didn't want to be that kiss-and-leave guy."

"What is holding you back now?"

He leans over and slowly kisses her on the right side of her neck. He places little soft pecks along her left cheekbone to her lips while his hands gently work their way through her hair. When both his hands are holding the back of her head, he nibbles on her lips. Then he gives her a deep passionate kiss on the mouth. Her legs quiver as the kiss goes on for minutes. They never told each other yet *I love you*, but with this kiss, they know without it being said.

She has never had a kiss like this. Soon she and Jack find themselves on the bridge floor making intimate love, rolling over and over each other as the clothes come off. She opens her eyes to see the moonlight just as everything ends in heavy breathing. They both have a tingling sense that this moment was special.

After getting dressed, the two walk over to his car and hold each other for a while.

"This is not how I wanted to leave. I did not want to say the words, *wait for me*, because what if I don't come back..."

She puts her fingers on his lips. "Shhhhh. I know that if you make it, you will do everything you can to find me here."

They do another slow and long kiss. He gets in the car and leaves as she stands there in the driveway, watching the last light of the taillights until they disappear. Jack stops at the end of the driveway, reaches down under the seat, and pulls out a little black box about three inches square. He opens the box that reveals a gold ring with a diamond heart, then he closes it and drives off.

Over the next few days, Brenda watches Daisy torture herself with worry that Jack might not make it back. Her friend's mood swings between happy and somber.

Daisy and Jack exchange letters through the winter months every two weeks until early March.

Unfortunate Timing

It's 10:30 am in Germany, and Jack is flying at 15,000 feet after the bombing run. He turns the squadron to fly back to England and slowly lowers altitude. He sees two bombers falling out of formation because of flak damage. He informs the crew they will fly with them to help provide cover while the rest of the group carries on.

Stateside, it's 4:30 am, Daisy is awakened by the phone ringing in the hallway. She makes her way out of bed and sleepy-eyed to answer it. She has been called in to work to deal with a nearby bus accident with multiple injuries, most of them soldiers.

***

10:38 a.m. Germany. Jack and his crew do everything possible to help save the other crews. There are too many fighters. He orders the failing planes to dive to the treetop level as quickly as they can. He will stay aloft to draw enemy fire. In a matter of minutes, his plane is riddled with bullets and flak that comes from the ground. His gunner crews are running out of ammo.

***

4:38 a.m. Stateside. Daisy starts her car and drives to the crash scene. In the darkness, she can see the lights over the next hill. Road dust and smoke reflect the light from the fire burning the grass and the bus. She parks partially off to the right side and gets out to see many people lying off the side of the road.

***

10:50 a.m. Germany. Bullets rip through the cockpit and through Jack's lower hip and legs. He yells in pain. An explosion outside the plane tilts it to the left. Jack orders the crew to bail out. His copilot doesn't budge. Jack yells for him to go, but he stays. Jack knows he can't move and wouldn't survive the jump even if he could. He tells his copilot he will hold the plane steady so all can get out. The copilot bids him a tearful, thankful good-bye.

***

4:50 a.m. Stateside. Daisy helps a soldier move off to the side of the road and goes back out to get another. A driver speeding over the hill sees the wreck too late and slams on the brakes. Tires squeal, the driver making every effort to stop the car, but it smacks Daisy hard. She flies into the air and seems to hang there for a split second before she falls to the dirt road, rolling over and over to end up on her left side. The car stops a foot away from her.

***

10:52 a.m. Germany. Jack uses all his strength to hold the plane upright. He looks out the left window and sees the other planes have made it to a safe flying level away from the fighters. He hears another explosion. Pieces of hot metal rip and tear through the flaming cockpit. The plane tilts more to the left. Jack is losing strength. He reaches into his pocket, pulls out a picture of Daisy, and wedges it between the yoke and his hands.

"I'm so sorry, Daisy. I should have told you I love you. You were the one for me all this time. I hope you will find someone to love you like I do."

***

4:52 a.m. Stateside. Daisy holds onto consciousness as best as she can despite extreme pain. She cannot move her legs. Her mouth is full of blood and her breathing is getting difficult. She knows she is dying.

"Oh Jack, my poor Jack. I should have told you I loved you. What are you going to do when you find out? I have never felt love like I had with you. I'm so sorry Jack."

***

10:55 a.m. Germany. Jack's plane starts to tumble wing over wing. Flames pour out of the craft while his crew watches from their opened parachutes gliding to the ground. He lets go of the yoke and holds her picture.

"Daisy, I love you so deeply, and you are part of my soul now. I am happy to have spent the time with you."

Jack's plane disintegrates into many pieces in the air from the tremendous explosion.

***

4:55 a.m. Stateside. A soldier comes over to help her along with Brenda who just arrived at the scene and is shocked to find Daisy barely alive. Her eyes fading, Daisy says, "I wanted us to be together forever, Jack. You seemed like a part of me. Tell him I love him too."

***

10:56 a.m. Germany. "I love you, Daisy."

***

4:56 a.m. Stateside. "I love you, Jack."

Closure for the New Beginning

Two buses stop at a farm lane in the Midwest on a late summer late afternoon. Ted, Brenda, and two other men get out of the first one, carrying a soldier's trunk. Ted makes a quiet gesture that they have the correct address and walks down the lane to the front porch. Brenda is wearing a bright red dress with a matching fedora, and the men are standing in their military dress uniforms. Ted steps up onto the porch, knocks on the door and steps back down.

Jack's father opens the door and instantly knows why they have had no mail from Jack in months. Jack's mother comes to the door sobbing. Ted steps up and speaks.

"Sir. I wanted to tell you in person and not have a telegram to say a few words. First, I want to say I am proud to have known Jack and had him as a squadron mate. He made us all better people. He took care of us and made sure we did our best to get everyone home. I also want to tell you about the days we were here stateside. All he could talk about was Daisy. How she made him feel all excited to see her again, even though he just left her. It wasn't infatuation, it was more like a deep desire to reclaim a love, he always said."

Brenda gives a handful of letters to Jack's mother.

"You must be Daisy," she says, trying to smile.

Brenda steps back, "No Ma'am. I am... was... Daisy's

best friend." She looks over at Ted to tell the story.

"We discovered something odd. Well, I don't know what to make of it. They both died on the same day, roughly at the same time, while being a continent apart."

Jack's mother gasps in amazement and cries. His father reacts quietly while looking at the trunk.

"This was Jack's belongings, sir," one man said.

"Daisy really loved Jack," Brenda says, continuing the story. "That is all she could talk about at the hospital where we worked. We were even joking about marriage plans. Daisy never told him she loved him, but she did madly and wanted to say it but thought it was too soon."

Ted clears his throat. "That was one of the last conversations we had, about how Jack wanted to tell Daisy he loved her."

"Jack was always a silent type and never really said anything 'til he was sure," his father says.

Ted continues on. "But sir. I wanted to say your son made the most incredible sacrifice over there." He explains how Jack used the plane to save his crew so they could jump out safely. He makes a motion for the others who had arrived on the buses to come forward.

"Sir, he didn't save just the lives of his crew. He gave himself up so these other men could come home to their families, their girls, their sons and daughters."

Jack's parents watch in utter amazement. Twenty-nine men in uniform come walking around the house from the lane and all stand in perfect rows behind Ted.

"Your son, Major Jack Flanders, saved the lives of these men. I am one of them. We could never repay that."

Ted stands back and salutes Jack's father. The rest of the men snap to attention and salute, too. Brenda hugs Jack's mother.

Jack's father is having trouble standing tall and wipes away a few tears working their way down his face.

"Thank you, good sir. It means a lot to us to hear all of that." He reaches out to shake Ted's hands.

***

Jack finds himself standing on a dirt road with cornfields to his left and right. The corn stalks are green and tall, and the aroma of sweet corn fills the air on a windless sunny day with puffy white clouds scattered about the sky. There is silence. No birds or cars or even tractors tending the fields. Jack looks down at himself dressed in his Army air force uniform, holding his cap under his left arm.

How can this be? He remembers his plane burning and falling out of the sky, but here he is standing on a dirt road. He recognizes this place as Daisy's uncle's farm lane in Gettysburg. Jack is not sure why, but he walks the lane toward the house. The thought of him burning in the plane quickly fades away, and so do most other memories, as he seems to be in a controlled daze.

He makes it to the top of the hill where the sweet corn turns into rows of apple trees. The apples are bright red and give off a strong delicious aroma. Over the hill is the white farmhouse with the barn sitting beside it and the little bridge that crosses the small stream. He sees the tree where Daisy and he carved their names into the trunk so their names would live on longer than they would.

Jack scoffs. *I never realized it would be that soon.* Jack is not sure why, but he should be heartbroken that he left or lost his love. *What will Daisy do now?* He turns around to see Daisy standing there in her white nurse's uniform with the sun on her back.

"This must be my imagination playing tricks on me."

"No Jack, it must be my mind playing tricks on me."

He walks over to Daisy, stands in front of her, and gazes into her beautiful yellowish green eyes. She stares back at him in that lost-in-you look she always gave him. He reaches out and pulls her tight into his chest. They stand there for a while and hold each other in the middle of the road.

"Oh Daisy, I'm pretty sure I've passed on. If this is the last memory I have, I want it to be about you."

Jack slowly grabs her chin, bends down, and gives her that slow, long kiss that he does so well. She holds his hands, pondering.

"Jack, I'm sure I have passed on as well. It was in a car wreck of some sort, and I ended up here watching you walk up to the tree."

They both look down at the farmhouse and can see someone sitting in an old rocking chair. Holding hands, they stroll toward the house. They get closer and see it is an old man wearing a dark blue Union soldier wool uniform, and he is whittling a stick, carving it to a point. They stop and glance at him.

"Who are you?" Jack asks.

The man smiles and takes the stick and points it toward the bridge. They both turn to see that the other side of the bridge is cloudy with a mist and not revealing anything.

Thus the man speaks. "Sometimes... just sometimes... people do amazing things. Acts of selflessness or caring for others at their own... sacrifice. But even rarer is when two people who are deeply in love with each other do that at the same… time. And that... that has caught the eye of someone... special... let's say."

He rocks the chair slowly. Jack and Daisy are still holding hands.

"What happens now?" Jack asks.

"You see... Your love is so strong for each other that the both of you never got the chance to live it to its fullest... again."

He swipes at the stick with his small knife and chips go flying off onto the ground.

"So go... go across the bridge. You are giving a... gift."

Again? A gift? Daisy and Jack are baffled as to what is happening.

"Go on. Time won't wait forever," the old man said.

The two of them make their way to the bridge. Jack stops halfway and holds Daisy again.

"I love you Daisy. I wanted to spend every day and night with you. Without you, I couldn't be."

He kisses her once more, then she says, "I love you too, Jack. And each day you were gone, my heart ached to have you back, hoping you would be okay."

The two of them disappear into the mist while the old man smiles, watching them.

"Yep, can't wait to see them again… Good people, they are. Hopefully next time they get to finish their journey."

***

Years go by until 2010, at the square in Gettysburg, almost as the sun is setting on a warm October day. A man about 30 years old, average build, short black hair, carrying his dark blue blazer jacket on his left arm walks down the sidewalk looking for a place to eat.

He stops at a small place called the Blue Parrot where a crowd outside is waiting for seating. It is a very old brick building. The brown tarp overhang shades the black metal graded tables and chairs. They are busy with customers having a good time. In the background, he can hear the plucking of a lonely guitar playing some blues song.

A brunette hostess stops by and says, "It will be about 15 minutes or so, sweetie."

Chills run up and down his body. He looks over the sidewalk across the street and gazes back at the hostess and says, "I will wait." All this looks familiar to him, yet he knows he has not been here.

He looks around, trying to figure out what this reaction is and locks eyes with a woman sitting at an outside table wearing a white sundress with red flowers. Her curly blonde hair shifts in the breeze. She is in a daze, staring at him while holding a drink in a tall thin glass. He smiles at her and she smiles back. He points at the empty seat. She welcomes him over with a nod of her head.

"Is this seat taken?"

Silence from the lady.

"Um, ma'am... You ok."

"That's so odd," she says. "Why do I think I know you?"

He looks at her. The accent goes straight through him as if he had heard that voice before. "Yes, something is very... odd feeling here," he says.

He shakes his head for a second.

"Hello, I'm Jake." He sits down and puts his jacket on the other empty chair. He looks at her for a moment. "Unless you've been to the Midwest, I couldn't possibly know you. This is my first time in Gettysburg and yet I feel as if I..."

She stares at his eyes and says, "My name is Lily." She looks over at his jacket and sees his wing emblem on it. "So, you are a pilot?"

Jake is about to say yes when her phone goes off. After the third ring, he points to it.

"Excuse me." Lily answers it. "Hello, Doctor Barnes

here. Ok, that will do. Make the appointment, please." She hangs up the phone and looks back at him. "Sorry about that."

"Yes."

"What?" she asks.

"Yes. I'm a pilot for a private corporation. And you're a doctor, I see."

Lily nods. "You were talking about a feeling?"

Jake blushes. "Well it's, um . . ." He rubs the bottom of his chin. "I don't know how to explain it."

He reaches out to hold her hand and stands up. Lily stands as well. "It's as if I've found you once more."

Lily tears up some. "Yes, as if I have missed you for a long time" she pulls him in to hug him... again.

An old man sits on a bench on the other side of the street, whittling a stick into something, and smiles. "Hopefully, they will get this right this time around."

Come follow him on the beginning journey of his story writing. Historical aviation fiction to fantasy adventure sagas.

He lives just outside of Gettysburg PA since 1997.

As a motorcycle enthusiast (owned a motorcycle service business), pilot and painter of things. Loves riding the country sides for view and ideas for stories. He is an aviation buff that enjoys flying in small planes atop the clouds to go for a dinner flight.

You can follow him or ask questions on Facebook @ Greg Spicka (one with planes and motorcycles on that page)

Check out my fantasy series at Tomesofauhere.com and the psychological thriller short story on Kindle, *The Girl in The Lemon Yellow Dress.*

Still Here

By Patricia Parks

The lot is weed-covered and filled with rubbish, some blown in, some clandestinely dumped. The realty sign, one of a series over the years, has been knocked down again and not righted. A hubcap glints in the weak sun, and a gray and white cat prowls in the ragweed, looking for some hapless small creature. The breeze blows plastic bags and last year's leaves into new arrangements on the broken asphalt. Nature is reasserting itself, but the winner is far from clear.

It used to be a busy, if not thriving, shopping center, with a Dollar General in the place of dubious pride, and multiple small shops and restaurants in a hopeful array around the generous parking area. I wondered if I was the only one who thought that, at least in Gettysburg, it should be called the General Dollar. My husband never laughed at this poor attempt at humor. He won't be laughing now. He sits, shoulders slumped, in an abandoned armchair, eyes closed, keeping his thoughts to himself as always. We haven't spoken out loud in at least a year. Seems we've said all we had to say.

I watch out my usual small window, furred with dust and webs from both active and long-deceased spiders, the corpses of their small conquests hanging limply, occasionally twisting in the stale air. The current owners added a layer of insulation to the attic, something we always meant to do but never got around to. They talk dispiritedly about further improvements, but so far it's just talk, unlikely to progress. They've stopped work on the second floor, and one bedroom there still has the paint we happily applied. It was called Optimist Yellow, but came out more of a garish egg-yolk shade. I was never gifted at color. The newest people did replace the windows there, getting rid of the vinyl ones we had installed throughout the house years ago. The seals had started to fail within a couple of years, and the milky glass always reminded us of our poor choice. But ill health and inflation ate up the funds we thought would outlast us, and we kept them, stubbornly covering them with shades.

We rarely go downstairs now. And nobody likes to come up here because of the bats clinging stubbornly to the rafters until twilight calls them on the hunt. Increasingly, going down just seems like a bother. And there's nothing new to hear; since their kids left, they have the same conversations with each other that we used to have. Too many are about money or its lack, how it doesn't go as far as it used to. They bought the place at a good price after the most recent bust, but their initial fizzing optimism gradually chipped away by the high costs of renovating and maintaining an older house. He talks about selling in a hopeless way, knowing her views about having a stable and familiar place for the kids to visit if they ever come back to the East Coast. They go round and round like cats in a bag. I used to find it entertaining, but it got old.

I wish they had more company. When their kids were home they always had a houseful, with friends staying over, cousins visiting, neighbors dropping by with home-grown produce or barbeque invitations. But the kids moved away, too far to visit very often, and their friends were lured away by better climates or the chance of lower taxes or better jobs. We don't recognize the people walking by anymore. Haven't in a while.

Houses on the street started getting divided into two- or three-bedroom apartments, even the grand old Victorians that had pride of place on the avenue. Most of the larger trees are gone, done in by paving, road salt, or ever-more-exotic diseases and insects. The lawns are browning in the summer sun, and lawn care is not the priority it used to be. The garden club hasn't awarded a Garden of the Month here in years. The burned-out place up the block leaves a gap like a tooth missing, another rubble-filled lot accumulating its inevitable layer of debris. I turn to my husband to point this out, but his closed eyes stop me yet again.

We've always been a quiet couple. In the past I used to thoroughly enjoy eavesdropping on conversations when we went out, made easier by this taciturn man who accompanied me. Taking a position on an overheard argument was a common pastime. It got to the point where his infrequent comments were nearly unwelcome as I picked a side in a whispered argument or, with more well-behaved neighbors, guessed what the menu option might prove to be. This habit was great fun here at first, especially as the various owners' kids got into their teens. Secrets then are so close to the bone. I had forgotten.

It's been a long time since we saw or heard a teenager. I still remember my granddaughter's visits fondly, though as she got older they got less frequent. Our granddaughter would be an old woman now. Is her memory the binding that keeps us here? She used to like visiting us, shopping at the candy store on Baltimore Street and taking our books to the coffee shop on Chambersburg Street. We moved to Gettysburg to be closer to her. Where is she now? We danced at her wedding in 2039. It was our last dance.

My husband went first, succumbing to the same illness that plagued him for his last seven years. His spirits were not high for some time, and the same melancholy affects him now, even though he no longer has the pain to contend with. I joined him several years later, rather suddenly. We were shocked to find ourselves back here. Of all the beliefs I had evolved over the years, this eventuality had never occurred to me. There was no one to ask, no one who could hear us. There must be others, but we don't see them. We never have. Just each other.

At first it was fun to accompany the ghost tours around town, large groups optimistically following a hoop-skirted actress with a lantern and hoping for a glimpse of the Civil War sniper, the lingering shadow of a soldier longing for another type of peace. They're not here, though they were once. No one saw us, not that an elderly couple from the 2040's were what was being sought. None of our attempts to introduce a chill, an apparition, a flicker of movement or a whisper was successful, but we got a kick out of the idea that we were *right there* while the earnest folks peered into attics and corners as bidden and the skeptics scoffed in the back. A few people seemed to get uneasy and sense our presence, but for the most part we were ignored. That got hard. Being ignored is no more fun in death than it was in life.

Town changed gradually, as towns do. The businesses we remembered changed hands or left entirely, and new ones took their place. We found it impossible to visit the new ones, even ones we thought we'd like, like the bookstore on Chambersburg Street. We eventually realized we were tied to what we had known and limited to the areas and surroundings we had visited. And travel was out; we attempted to leave town once, to visit where our son used to live, and it did not go well. There really should be a handbook for this, like in that old movie. What was its name? No idea anymore.

Then the house started to confine us. Lately even visiting the kitchen feels like an effort. We've retreated, room by room, until we're nearly always up here. Why the attic? I wonder. We rarely entered it before, and now it's the only place we're relatively comfortable in.

I look at my hands, scanning for a trace of the transparency I both dread and wish for, the beginning of yet another inevitable end. Can I see the pattern from the old armchair through my husband's all-too-familiar attire? Does he long for this next phase to begin? Even if we wanted to, we can't go far from the house now without becoming shaky. Daylight or dark, it doesn't matter.

Our deaths were little ones, not part of a famous battle or a dramatic encounter. But we linger, as long as we have ties to the world. I believe those ties are fading. Change must come, and even we can't stay the same.

Drive up toward what remains of the Seminary, past the vacant lot. and go slowly. Look in the third floor windows if you can. You won't see us, but I'll see you. And I doubt we're alone. What you seek is likely different; but what remains has some substance at least. For now.

Pat Parks is a recent transplant to Gettysburg from a small town in upstate New York. She is a retired librarian, a proofreader, owned a used bookstore, and reads voraciously. Sense a theme? She found the Gettysburg Writers Brigade almost immediately and attended a meeting before moving into her current home. She loves fantasy, science fiction and occasionally dabbles in reality.

A Friend for Life

By Felicia Valasek Rizzo

In loving memory of Chloe

I sat on a bench in Unity Park facing Baltimore Street, staring intently at the Historic Farnsworth House Inn. Recalling all of the tales I have told over the years to thousands of visitors, I felt melancholy. I loved being a ghost tour guide in Gettysburg. Telling the history, dramatizing the legends, enjoying the camaraderie were all part of the fun. Oh, how I miss it. I'm not even sure why. I just know that I do.

A jovial, pleasantly plump woman in period dress sat down beside me. It was a hot day as she waved her lace fan to and fro as she gave herself some relief from the humidity.

"This is quite a surprise," she stated with a smile on her face.

"Pardon?"

"Seeing you here at this hour. I usually see you pass by in the evenings telling your splendid tales of old."

"Oh? I'm sorry. I haven't seen you before. I'm assuming you are another tour guide, then?"

"You could say that," she chuckled.

We made some more small talk, sharing ghost stories. Mostly, we sat in a comfortable silence just watching the people pass us by. Every now and then, a child would look our way and smile, usually with ice cream from Mr. G's dripping down their chubby chins. Some adults would look our way, unsettled. Others snapped pictures of the lady in the long black and purple dress from the 1800's who was sitting beside me.

As it grew dusk, tourists started to gather in the park for one of the many ghost tours offered here in town. Guides in period garb carrying lanterns and adjusting their speaker-phones rushed by us to check people in for their tours. The park started to get rather congested. I preferred when it wasn't so crowded.

I quietly got up and bid the nice woman good-bye. She gave a slight wave, a big smile, then told me she would see me tomorrow. I found that rather odd. How would she know that she would see me tomorrow? Then I remembered I used to give ghost tours here every day and she did mention she had seen me each day. I didn't bother to tell her that it seemed like forever since I'd given my last tour. I turned to walk past Mr. G's, one of the witness trees, then on down Baltimore Street toward the town square. I never understood why they called it "the square" when it is a circle after all.

As I strolled, I thought to myself, "Boy, I could walk this path with my eyes closed by now and not trip over an uprooted sidewalk." There was a time when I would have tripped multiple times if I didn't have my lantern on full brightness watching every step that I took. The sidewalks were quite uneven on Baltimore Street. I always had to tell my guests to please watch their step and show them the way. How many times had I taken this same walk? Every day, sometimes two or three times a day, over the ten years I've lived here. I loved my tours so much that I hated to take a day off.

As I arrived home to my little apartment on North Washington Street, I could see my sweet bichon, Chloe, peering through the glass pane in the door. She wagged her tail profusely, anxiously waiting for me to walk through the door, as she propped herself up on her hind legs and paddled her front paws on the door in excitement. Upon picking her up, my face was immediately covered in doggy-kisses. My favorite kind. I set her down, so we could walk outside off the little porch, into the grassy area behind our building. I used to have to put a leash on her or she would be curious about everything and run. I no longer did that. She stayed right beside me.

After Chloe sniffed around, we went back inside the apartment. The television turned itself on as I was making a pot of decaf. Chloe let out a yelp. I abruptly turned to see the History channel come to life. At least our resident ghost had good taste. I left the TV on and sat down on the sofa to enjoy my steaming cup of joe with Chloe upon my lap as stories of World War II filled the screen.

I must have dozed off because when I awoke, the sun was streaming through the curtains, the television was off and the bed was made. Chloe was running around in circles impatiently getting my attention for her daily walk. We started in the grassy area outside of our door. Next, we made our way up to Seminary Ridge where we walked along the pathways on the United Theological Seminary campus. This was our daily routine. Chloe always stayed right beside me, looking up and smiling with her tongue out on our whole walk. I always worried that she would overheat, but I always took a water bottle with me for her to drink.

When we returned, I fed her. Then we were back outside for her to sniff around and do her business, and back inside we went. At some point, I ended up on the park bench just staring at the Farnsworth House. Some days someone new might show up. Like the kind woman who joined me yesterday. I'm not sure how this became my routine, but it has. I've embraced it. Yet, I feel this longing to give tours again. That is why I come here. At least, I think that is why I come here. I am not even sure why I don't give the tours anymore. I'm beginning to think I'm depressed again. I'm forgetful. I have lapses of time. I'm quiet. I don't spend time with anyone anymore, just Chloe.

"Hello, again." The jovial woman once again appeared, wearing the same thing as yesterday.

"Hello," I said with a smile, as I moved over for her to join me.

"Not quite as muggy as yesterday, thank goodness."

"I hadn't really noticed. No, it's not. Which company do you work for?" I asked to make friendly conversation.

"Oh, I work for myself. Shh…" She put a finger up to her lips looking around. "Don't tell anyone that. They don't take too kindly to people like me around here. I give my own tours."

"You do? No one has ever said anything?"

Giving tours in Gettysburg was serious business. You had to be licensed with the borough and have your permit and license shown at all times. It was a cutthroat business, too. Town meetings were always being held with some competitor complaining about another.

She just laughed "I've had a few people try to tell me to take a hike. I'm here to stay. I was born and raised here. My family goes back generations to the founding fathers of this town- the Gettys'. What are they going to say to me?" she asked proudly with a shoo of her hand. "I'll tell you another thing, the likes of some behavior I have seen in this town would have my granddaddy rolling in his grave. Sometimes, I go up to Black's Graveyard and have chats with him." She paused. "I probably sound like a crazy person to you."

"Not at all. I find peace in graveyards and cemeteries. I've been known to speak to the dead a time or two myself. No judgement here."

"I'm sure you do," she said as she patted my knee.

The park, once again, began to get crowded. Once again, I got up at dusk to make my way back home. This time, I gave a gentle wave to my new friend as I headed north on the uneven sidewalk toward the square, toward Chloe.

"See you tomorrow," she called out.

Day after day, week after week, I fell into the same routine. I woke up, walked with Chloe, found myself on the park bench chatting with my new friend, watched the park get crowded at dusk, went home, snuggled Chloe, then found that I had dozed off.

Then one day, my new friend suggested something different.

"Hello!"

"Hello," I reply. I had begun to really like this routine.

"I have an idea. Let's do something else!"

I patiently waited for her to tell me what her idea was.

"Since we both like to give tours, let's give each other a tour. I think it's time," she said matter of factly.

"You mean, I will take you on the tour that I would give then you take me on yours?"

"Something like that," she smiled and nodded her head. "What do you say?"

"Sure. I think I would like that. Would you like to go first?"

"How about you go first? I know you would give your tours starting from this location and we are already here."

We stood, turned to the left, and made our way to the Brickhouse Inn and the Welty House. I shared the story of a Confederate soldier telling a woman to keep her head down as she looked out the window onto Baltimore Street. I then pointed across the street to the John Rupp house and told tales of unseen children tugging on people's clothes and how the home was riddled with so many bullets that the owner could scoop up the shells with both hands. I elaborated how a soldier was found dead in the Rupp's garden and how other soldiers who died on the lawn were buried right where they lay.

We then ventured up to the Jennie Wade house where I told a heart-wrenching story of the young woman who was the only civilian to die during the Battle of Gettysburg. We moved on to the orphanage where a child was locked up in a shed in the freezing winter, with no clothes, starving and how some children never leave.

We ventured back down toward Unity Park where I told tales of the Farnsworth House which many claim to be a portal for spirits. Heading north we made a stop at the Tillie Pierce Inn where a woman claims to have seen a young girl change into something hideous and checked out early, never to return.

As I told my stories, my new friend listened with fascination. She became wide-eyed at some tales, laughed at others, but always asked questions with genuine interest. She was a wonderful tour guest and it brought back so many fond memories and how much I had loved my job.

When I finished at the police station, having told about

Gus the ghost who still likes to cook even after death, with the smell of chili wafting through the hallways tantalizing those that work there currently, she folded her hands and thanked me for a wonderful tour. She then asked me if I was ready for hers. I was eager to hear her stories, for I knew she would be a wonderful storyteller! I said yes, and we moved along heading toward the square.

My new friend told me of the ghost of the Gettysburg Hotel. Where a woman in white is said to roam the hallways and the ballroom. We moved down Carlisle Street, then left to Gettysburg College. Oh, the stories she told at the college! The most fascinating was the story of staff in Pennsylvania Hall being taken down to the basement in an elevator and when the doors opened, it was as if they were back in time, seeing a grisly scene of soldier amputations as they valiantly pushed buttons for the doors to close! I believe we were at the college for a full hour. She could have gone on and on, but it was past dusk and I needed to get to Chloe to take her out. I told her so.

She smiled softly and said she had one more story to tell, an important one. We turned right out of the campus and onto North Washington Street. My street. As we got to my building she stopped and looked at the red brick colonial then at me.

"My final story is here."

"Here? This is where I live. I knew it was haunted!"

There was Chloe at the door, wagging her tail, up on two legs pawing at the glass pane. I asked if she minded if I left my pup out while she told her tale. She smiled, reached down and patted Chloe on the top of her head as soon as I let her out. Chloe stayed right by my side, sniffing at the grass.

"Do you mind if I ask what you've experienced here before I tell my story?" she asked.

"The usual haunting occurrences. The television and lights will go off and on by themselves. Cabinets and doors will open. I will hear footsteps. Things will get moved around. Is there something bad here I should be aware of?"

Just then Chloe barked for attention, wanting to be held. I scooped her up into my arms and looked back at the woman in the black and purple period dress about to tell me a story of my home. A story I wasn't sure I wanted to know.

A few college students passed by us emanating a shiver. At ninety-plus degrees on a summer night, some could still feel the chill of the dead or a haunted place. This was Gettysburg, the land itself was haunted.

I looked at my friend and implored her to go on, unsure if I would be able to sleep that night.

"The story I am about to tell happened not that long ago. A young woman had just gotten back to her apartment on the first floor after giving a ghost tour."

She had my full attention as I held my bichon a tad bit tighter.

"It was about midnight. She had made herself a pot of coffee, turned on the TV, and snuggled up on her sofa with her sweet pup, just like yours." She turned to look me straight in the eye before she softly smiled and looked to the left before she continued. "Three men were arguing in the parking lot, what would later be revealed as a dispute over a drug deal gone bad. Shots were fired. The young woman heard the shots and immediately called 911. The men were right outside her apartment window. One man was yelling at another to go, when her dog started barking. Two young men fired straight into the window killing the young woman and her dog instantly."

I gasped, horrified at hearing this news. "When did this

happen?"

"Two years ago. Tonight."

"That couldn't be. I would have been living here."

Then it registered, and I gasped for air, choking back sobs. Clutching Chloe, I fell to my knees. My new friend knelt down beside me, cradling me with one arm and stroking Chloe with her other hand. Chloe licked the tears from my face and nuzzled in deeper to comfort me.

"A man lives here now. Says the place is haunted. He tells of hearing footsteps around midnight and the pitter-patter of little paws. Things are moved, doors and cabinets open and close. Lights and the television turn on by themselves."

She helped me back to my feet.

"What do I do now?" I asked. "Now that I'm a ghost," I whispered.

"Whatever you wish. Some choose to stay for their own reasons. Me? I stayed to help others like you. Others go on to the light to meet their loved ones and wait for those yet to arrive. It is all up to you."

We hugged each other tight.

As I slipped through the door, I turned back to thank my new friend. She was already gone as a ghost tour was arriving at the front of the house to tell my story.

Felicia Valasek Rizzo is an aspiring writer and author of a novel that is still in progress. An elementary school teacher for the past decade and a half, she has shared her love of stories, reading, writing, and history with future generations. As a native of Kittanning, Pennsylvania, she has often wandered off fulfilling her wanderlust living in various parts of the East Coast while road tripping across the country. Someday soon she hopes to settle in Gettysburg, the setting of her debut historical fiction narrative. As an amateur historian of the Battle of Gettysburg, she explores and researches differing aspects of this great pivotal moment in our Nation's history. As a member of the Friends of Gettysburg and the American Battlefield Trust she hopes to keep history alive, so we never forget, nor repeat our ancestors' fates. In her free time, Felicia enjoys attending historical lectures, especially about the Civil War – most importantly – Gettysburg.

She Walks Through Dreams

BY KERRY SPRINGLE

Dreaming... all of the voices that I hear in my head are really more than just the souls I have met, talking still. They are anyone's and everyone's that I get close to. They are stories; I hear their stories. The humans call some of them dreams.

Part One

This all started because I wanted to see what a Starbuck tasted like. I came back to Gettysburg for the "reenactment" weekend and kept hearing the humans talking about them, saw them carried with both hands wrapped around like the things are a life force or something. As if an actual life force would fit into even a grande size. When I was here for the battle in 1863 I never heard a mention of Starbucks.

Well, I can now say that they don't taste anything like the stardust I've had, and mermaids don't ever go around with two tails (that's a common procedure now to have one removed), and the hot wet part tasted worse than the deepest sea water I've drunk. I will say, the holder part that works like a chalice wasn't bad if I held it on my tongue for a bit before chewing. It sort of melted in my mouth. Even after all of this time and energy trying to understand what they crave about them, I will not stand in line waiting to try again.

Before I started escorting just humans, I walked all over the universe finding souls and taking them to my boss. I have been walking around worlds, finding the ready souls, for so long now that I don't even remember when I started. Father Time jokes with me each time I complete the circumference of a planet that I should be flying rather than walking, pulling gently on his floor-length white beard as is his habit and nodding his white tufted head in the direction of my very obvious raven-black wings. But, I don't like to fly, I like to explore and experience the places that I visit. Flying is so unhuman, and since I began walking the earth I enjoy trying to be as much like the humans as I can. I am intrigued by them. This world is the most interesting and fast; it has the most souls needing an escort, so I am kept busy enough to make the excuse to stay around here most of the time.

I guess to explain my job more thoroughly, I have seen cats and dogs do it also, laying the prizes of their hunt at the feet of their master. I hear a soul's last story start in my head like someone is reading it to me, and I go and find them. I tell them that I will assist them with finding their way to the next adventure. I love that word, "adventure." I learned it from the humans and it sounds so much more appealing than "the next realm" or "next soul journey" or "afterlife."

They react to me like I am giving them a choice, tilting their head to one side as if pondering their options, even though we both know they will be walking with me. They often begin to tell me many more of their stories as we go, unaware that I hear them all when we get physically close to one another. It surprises them to hear me say things that I shouldn't know, and pick up telling the story they are beginning to tell me. I smile calmly in response to their look of amazement or confusion. Then I proceed to tell them about where we are heading toward.

I suppose that you would like to know who I am, wouldn't you? I am just a black shadow floating around this big frightening world, at times terrified myself, mostly unseen by humans unless I choose to be. I am the delivery service for souls from one life to their next, just like all of my female ancestors have been. I am a scanner, continuously curious about everything I encounter in this world and all the others. I am a writer, because after learning about that job around a thousand years ago, I have finally started calling myself one. I am Riga, a harbinger of doom.

My grandmother called me Riga when I was born and that became my name of sorts, at least when I am among the humans. I am the youngest of a long line of Morrigans, or shapeshifting dark goddesses, death doulas, whose real job description is a conduit of souls from this world to their spirit one.

Many Morrigan families will take the form of crows, but mine has always shifted to ravens, and we traditionally haunt battlefields reminding warriors that their body is temporary, and we will help their soul to its portal of transformation.

We can shapeshift to anything we choose to, if we concentrate well enough. My human form is the most difficult to maintain, there are so many details to get correct. I try to mimic their movements and speed, which adds to the complexity. I have found, after hundreds of years, that I don't have to hide my large black wings as the humans don't seem to worry about them, which is very helpful. I have found that my long thin black hair can be shocking at times as I have not found many humans with deep black like mine. My colors just seem all wrong for this world as it changes with time. In my opinion my ivory skin looks as old as it is, more fit for the Victorian era, especially now when I see how the younger females slather on potions to keep themselves from aging. I also find that when I have my wings covered I am often mistaken for one of the vampires. While it is a reasonable mistake, I do not sparkle as they do, only shimmer in the light.

My long black hair, the silvery blue hint on my skin, smoke gray eyes, and my tendency to soften and blur my edges when I get anxious, along with the wings, makes me less than able to blend in a crowd. Except, I tend to fade into a shadow when I get nervous, so that can be helpful when I find myself stuck in a mass of humans and start to get overwhelmed by all of their stories playing in my mind all at once.

During the 1863 battle I was concentrating on a Union infantry soldier moving stealthily from one fallen body to the next. I started to shift to his likeness so that I could follow behind and assist the dying in my way. When he moved to the edge of the field and stood to lean against a tree to rest, he reached up and removed his cap and I suddenly realized that he was a she! I slowly made my way to her, watching as she let her black hair come loose from its knot that had helped to hide it, and must have been gaping. She noticed me moving slowly toward her and smiled at me and said, "Surprise."

She thought I was alarmed at her being female, but I had met female warriors in plenty of wars all over the planet. I had been gaping at her black hair. "Your hair is gorgeous," I stammered out, as I self-consciously touched my own.

She smiled sheepishly, wiping field dirt, blood and tears from her prettily featured face, and looked off into the distance as if not seeing the field of carnage that looked like a poorly painted still life rendering of tragedy before us, "That black hair is the only part of home I've got left. Everything else went up in flames."

"So you came here to fight as one of them? Was this for revenge?" Since I had become distracted I had shifted back to my own form, and my wings flicked slightly as they always do when I'm uncomfortable.

She looked directly into my face and said in a hollow quiet voice, "This battle looks like nothing when compared to the destruction I've seen. Here they fight with weapons as if being gentlemanly, but my village and home was set on fire, slowly and intentionally. I ran out of our burning farmhouse straight toward him, thinking he was there to help. I looked up into his fiery eyes, and after he stared back into mine for a minute, as if he recognized me, he just turned and flew away. He let me live." We both shuddered, her at her memories and me at the recognition.

Part Two

I have enjoyed the many varied and beautiful environments while wandering this world, much more varied and colorful than some of the other worlds I have visited, and the inhabitants here are much more varied and colorful too. I have always enjoyed this world's ocean and sea floors the most as well, they are quite peaceful places to wander when the stories become overwhelming. The waters are full of creatures using languages that are ancient on this planet, and beautifully soothing compared to the ones the humans have been babbling for so long now.

The humans use their languages to show me what all of the emotions look like that they write so many storybooks about. They wear these emotions on their faces most of the time, but they often use their hands and bodies to express them. I am able to also sense heat and cold coming off of the humans who use some of the stronger ones. I find that I enjoy witnessing many, particularly the sounds of laughter (for the joy and happy emotions), which is like a new style of music. I really would like to understand what makes them decide to use certain emotions at certain times. There are so many, and I don't sense that there are any real rules about their use. The most confusing aspect is that different humans wear and use emotions differently.

I have always thought of myself as a black soul, heartless and incapable of any type of human behavior aside from being endlessly curious, but I am finding that as the decades pass less people seem afraid and more are curious about me. Recently though, since I started writing my book, I have been finding out that my black soul is actually full of colors. I have been choosing to spend time out among them, listening, to see if I can find any similarities between myself and any of them. My stories are so different from theirs that I never feel like they can understand about me, but I have encountered some who are able to think bigger than the lives they currently walk in. Their stories feel like they are from far away. These stories are the dreams.

I have been reading so many books, all different types of books, to try and learn what the humans record as descriptions of the emotions. Humans love books. I mean, they've been devoting buildings to them all over the planet for centuries, "libraries" are what they call most of them. Most of those structures are bigger and more elaborate than the ones they call "home," sometimes housing thousands of books, so it leads me to assume the books are valuable.

While visiting many large homes to collect souls, I have seen smaller versions of the libraries. There have been elaborate ones with places to sit and read a book by a fire, or to write a book at a table. The earth is scattered with other grand buildings for other types of treasures as well, but it seems that the treasures humans find most worth dying for are usually left lying on ocean and sea floors. Because of this it appears to me that the books are most valuable to them.

Some of these collection buildings, all around the world, even have people with weapons standing guard, making sure that the words stay in the books. I prefer these buildings, they are quiet and smell good, it is the smell of time. My preferred books are thick and heavy, full of people's dreams. When I read them I am able to stop hearing the constant sound of the stories that are always trying to be loudest in my head.

After spending hundreds of years roaming the libraries of this world, I have decided to write a book. I like the idea that one of the smiling ladies who roam the book buildings, making sure to keep the people reading so that their stories stay quiet for me, will put my book on a shelf with all of her others to keep it safe. I will finally have something valuable then to show as mine.

After a full day reading I had placed a heavy leather volume on a cart for the book lady, and was walking out of the Gettysburg library smiling to myself. I had just made up my mind to try writing my story. I had just stepped through the front doors and I made eye contact with a petite dark haired woman standing in the entryway, and she was wearing a perplexed expression and looking as if she wasn't sure about going out or coming in. She was holding a Starbuck, and she was beautiful, with radiant emerald green eyes and a row of soft freckles that lined the tops of her flushed cheeks. In the same breath we both spoke. I asked if she was alright, and she said that my smile was magical. Our eyes held each others' for the briefest of moments, and then she took some of my magic.

I had not felt that loss or connection with anyone from this world, and I felt like the air had been pulled up out of my lungs through my mouth. I watched my magic pull in a shimmery iridescent white line from my face, like an exhaled breath, and travel across the space between us to find her. It joined with her energy which was vibrating in her agitation, and changed its color to a green similar to her eyes as it transitioned.

As I stood motionless in front of her, trying to understand what had just occurred and also how to react, she smiled slightly and put a hand on my shoulder, "That didn't hurt, did it? I haven't really done that before, you are my first connection."

"I'm a connection? Connected to what? I don't know what just happened or what you are speaking of."

"Yes, a connection, I took a fragment of your magic so that I can connect to your frequency. I suppose that is the best way to say it. Now I can feel your energy and assist when you are in need." At my puzzled expression she pulled at my arm and guided me back into the library.

As we headed toward the old stairwell at the back of the building I must have had a puzzled expression and she explained, "I am going to show you where I work. This will explain why you have never seen me in the library even though I am very aware that you visit here often. I am this region's Enchantment librarian, in charge of the master collection of magic and otherworldly subject materials. My name is Sigilla, you can call me Sig, but please do not call me Gil."

When I tried to hide my wide-eyed smirk she responded, "my older siblings teased me by calling me Gil and I have never been able to hear that without wanting to throw a book at them." She clenched her small fists and blew out a breath, "The books get really angry if they are mishandled, so I just stomp my foot instead." She pulled her jacket off and turned to hang it on the back of her desk chair, which gave me my first sight of her fairy wings. "We have so much to talk about, but I know that you have your writing group tonight. Will you be sharing your story with them as you planned?"

In response to my stiffened posture and gasp of amazement at her knowing about my plans at the writing group, and especially about my story, she whispered, "When I took your magic I learned quite a bit about you, but don't worry, I am bound to keep your secrets safe just as if they are mine." Her smile was radiant and a bit mischievous as she moved a pile of books from her desk to a nearby work table.

I nodded an affirmative response to her raised eyebrow and crossed arms as she turned to me expecting an answer. "Yes, I am going to share a little of my story tonight. I am a bit nervous though, I have never shared any of it nor read in front of others before. I am not sure how they will respond since most of them have at least a few books already on the shelves here, well, there," and I pointed up to the library above us.

Sigilla glanced up as if able to see those volumes on the shelves above us. Then she glanced around her office and then landed her gaze on another door opposite of the one we had come in through. She took a step toward it, but then hesitated, "Maybe the tour will be best tomorrow, I don't want to take your attention from your reading tonight. Can you come and spend some time with me tomorrow and I will explain more of what we will be working on as I show you around the Enchantment library, introduce you to the volumes?"

I was already shaking my head excitedly up and down, "Of course, I am so curious to find out what you do and what this has to do with me. Will you taking some of my magic affect how I use it? Will I still have all of my powers? Do you now have my powers?" All of this came out in a flurry of thoughts.

"No, I will not have any of your magic, but I will be able to understand it and know what to pull from the books to assist you when you need to use it. You still have all of your magic and it works just the same, only now I will be your scholar to help you use ancient magic as well. We will talk tomorrow and I will explain it all, alright?" She smiled gently as she turned me toward the door that we had come in through and walked with me to the bottom of the iron spiral staircase leading back to the surface library. "Good luck tonight, I will be there to hear you read. You will be terrific!"

As she continued to smile and waved her small hand I started to ascend the stairs while still looking back at her. I must have looked perplexed still because she chuckled and said up the stairs after me, "Tomorrow, I promise."

I walked through the library, breathing in the scent of the books, and as I stepped out into the late afternoon warmth I felt a tingle of anticipation about what tomorrow would mean for me. I then remembered my story, patted my back pocket to feel the papers folded there, and walked down the stairs wondering if I should try another Starbuck to give me courage.

Kerry Springle kills people, in her murder mystery stories, and is currently constructing a novel of another design.

She holds a Master's degree in Library Science from Clarion University of Pennsylvania. She currently works as a Scientific Communications Specialist at a pharmaceutical company.

She spends time with her two teenagers, and her free time painting, creating, camping, and exploring as much of the world as she is able.

You can find her on Instagram *@emrawmama.*

ARE YOU AN AUTHOR OR INTERESTED IN WRITING?

Be a part of the Gettysburg Writers Brigade

We meet every Wednesday evening at O'Rorke's Restaurant in Gettysburg. It's a fun evening filled with writing discussions and friendship among fellow writers. You can attend occasionally or every week, whatever works for your schedule.

Join our Meetup.com group to get meeting notices: *www.meetup.com/Gettysburg-Writers-Brigade-Meetup-Group/*

You can also follow us on Facebook at: *www.facebook.com/groups/435601707040338*

Made in the USA
Middletown, DE
24 November 2023